God's
01/19/12

The Two Keys
To The Kingdom Of God

Sis Davis,
May the LORD bless,
guide and keep you
in 2012 and forever
in Jesus Name.

Pastor Charles

The Two Keys To The Kingdom Of God

Dr. Emeka O. Ozurumba

Copyright © 2009 by Dr. Emeka O. Ozurumba.

Library of Congress Control Number: 2009910284
ISBN: Hardcover   978-1-4415-8557-8
           Softcover   978-1-4415-8556-1

All rights reserved. No part of this book may be reproduced or transmitted in any form or by any means, electronic or mechanical, including photocopying, recording, or by any information storage and retrieval system, without permission in writing from the copyright owner.

Scripture taken from the New King James Version®. Copyright© 1992 by Thomas Nelson, Inc. Used by permission. All rights reserved.

Scripture quotations marked "AV" are taken from the Authorized King James Version®. Copyright©2003 by Thomas Nelson, Inc. Used by permission. All rights reserved.

This book was printed in the United States of America.

To order additional copies of this book, contact:
Xlibris Corporation
1-888-795-4274
www.Xlibris.com
Orders@Xlibris.com
66188

Contents

Preface 9
Acknowledgment 11

THE TWO KEYS TO THE KINGDOM OF GOD

Introduction 15
My Conversion Testimony 19
The Spiritual Foundations To The Keys 23
Chapter One: The Foundation Of Spiritual Repentance 27
Chapter Two: The Foundation Of Spiritual Agreement 41
Chapter Three: Are You Truly Born Of
   God And Risen With Christ? 51
Chapter Four: The Spiritual Characteristics
   Of Born Of God 55
Chapter Five: We Are What We Do, Not What We Say 69
Prelude To The Two Keys 75

LOVE: THE FIRST KEY TO THE KINGDOM OF GOD

Chapter Six: The Spiritual Hunger For God 81
Chapter Seven: Love For Others 91
Chapter Eight: The Tests of Love of Others 105

Chapter Nine: Where Two or Three Are
    Gathered In His Name 115
Chapter Ten: The Foundation Of
    Spiritual Forgiveness For Others 123
Chapter Eleven: The True Spiritual Forgiveness 133
Chapter Twelve: The Foundation Of
    Spiritual Reconciliation 138

OBEDIENCE:
THE SECOND KEY TO THE KINGDOM OF GOD

Chapter Thirteen: Obedience (Obey) 149
Chapter Fourteen: The Mystery Of
    The Burden Of Joshua 156
Chapter Fifteen: The Greatest Spiritual Victory 160
Chapter Sixteen: The Mystery Of Judah,
    The Son Of Jacob 171
Chapter Seventeen: The Blessings Of The Two Keys 178
Chapter Eighteen: What Else? 183

Index 195

DEDICATION

To the glory of God.

Preface

While millions of us (Christians) profess to be born again of God, very few understand and comprehend what it actually means to be truly born of God and transformed into His holy image. The common misconception among us is that once we leave one traditional denomination or church to a Pentecostal church, or once we proclaim Jesus as Lord and Savior, standing alone transforms us to born-again creatures. As a result of this misconception and misbelief, many are building on false foundation while others are outrightly deceived. And yet it is written, "Most assuredly, I say to you, unless one is born again, he cannot see the kingdom of God" (Jn 3:3). A total transformation into the image of the Son means being one and fused together in agreement with Jesus. As Jesus is one with the Father, so those who are born of Him ought to be one with the Father and the Son; for it is written, "Can two walk together, unless they are agreed" (Am 3:3).

This is a true statement that must sink in: Those who are born of God are the sons of God, and being sons of God, they are gods and spirits of God. "That which is born of the flesh is flesh, and that which is born of the Spirit is spirit" (Jn 3:6).

This is the kingdom's message, and this book will stir up the children of God to properly take stock of their present standing and relationship with God, as well as bring clarity and understanding of the concept of being born again of God. It highlights the urgency for us to return to the love of the truth according to the Gospel and doctrine of Jesus Christ as the coming of the Lord is nearer than ever. The book is filled with occasions of uncompromising hard truth in strict obedience to the directives of the Holy Spirit. With that, this book is particularly suited for all those who are most desirous and determined to enter the divine rest of God. The elect of God are given to understand the mysteries of the kingdom and appreciate the bitter truth, which is life and spirit. I therefore invite you to join me in unveiling the mysteries of the two keys to the kingdom of God.

Acknowledgment

I owe great gratitude and debt to many wonderful people who vigorously urged and pressed for the book to be written and helped and encouraged me during the writing and preparation of the manuscript. The book owes its existence to a great number of people: to my beloved wife, partner, and friend, Ugochi Katherine Ozurumba, for her unyielding love, faithfulness, dedication, and support throughout the book project, as well as for enduring over three and half years of rigorous evangelical work in Nigeria with me; Deborah "Queen Raven" J. Larsen, for graciously providing my necessities from the beginning to date and for the assistance and encouragement in the preparation of the manuscript. Your unparalleled unselfish love, friendship, and care are all unique and divine; Dr. James O. Okorafor, who encouraged me in every way and also assisted in the typing of the manuscript; Dr. James Arthur, Mazi Benson Okoronkwo, M. L. Copenhaver, Bonaventure Okereafor, and Johnny Nosike, for their encouragement; Mary Lou Kopech and Debbie Nunley, for their selfless assistance in typing the manuscript; the many pastors and members of various congregations who have asked and encouraged that the teachings be put in a book format; members of Today Evangelical

Ministries Bible Study Fellowship both in USA and Nigeria, for their love and support and, above all, their uncompromising commitment and dedication to the truth of the Gospel of Jesus Christ; the many friends and supporters, including A. G. Usman (fondly called my brother), whom God has used, one way or another, to support, assist, and encourage me, I am very humbly grateful. May God greatly enrich your knowledge of Him and bless and prosper the works of your hands.

THE TWO KEYS TO
THE KINGDOM OF GOD

Introduction

I thank God that this book is finally in the hands of readers like you. So many brothers and sisters of the Lord have been mounting pressure for a while that I commit to writing in a book format the teachings and mysteries the Lord revealed to me. Hence, the idea of this book came as a result of the promptings of the Holy Spirit, the revelations God gave to many, and the urging of ministers and members of different congregations the Lord has graciously allowed me to minister to.

Permit me to state from the onset that this book is a teaching inspired by the Spirit of God and based strictly on personal encounter, experience, and revelations of the mysteries of God's kingdom. With that, the reader will quickly notice that there is not a single reference to any book other than the Holy Bible. This should not be perceived as a demonstration of my inability to conduct intensive research of the many books written by respected Christian authors, but rather in deference to a higher voice. Moreover, there is no greater research material than the Holy Bible. For in truth, that which is written is written.

It is my strong belief that this book is made available at God's appointed time for the preparation of the saints for the coming of the Lord. It is also intended to pull down all the idols in our hearts and all the false imaginations and manipulative strongholds, deceit, and lies that are permeating and strangling the body of Christ today. It is my sincere prayer that God will use this book to remove the scales off the eyes of His elect, with the sole purpose of getting them to return to the love of the truth-first love. The enemy has succeeded for long in getting many ministers of the Gospel to turn blind eyes and deaf ears to the truth of the Gospel and doctrine of our Lord and Savior, Jesus Christ—all for their own selfish and covetous gains. It is now a rush for the number game. While perfecting various cunning devices and "Psychology 101 feel good" doctrine and preaching, they strife and compete viciously to keep their kingdoms. And what with most members with itching ears to hear what they want to hear, they strive to please people while compromising and watering down the word of life.

There are millions who profess and believe that they are born again of God but lack the understanding; neither do they have the comprehension of what it actually means to be born of God. As such, most of us believe falsely that we are ready now to meet the Lord. It is therefore imperative for all of us (Christians) to pause and take an urgent and serious self-examination of the true state of our relationship with God to ascertain whether we have ever been in agreement with Him, and if so, are we still walking within the course and scope of the original master plan? To do so, one needs to go back to the basic to trace the relationship. Hence, this book opens with the foundation of eternal life. "Repent, for the kingdom of heaven is at hand" (Mt 3:2, 4:17). Unless a builder builds on a solid foundation, he builds in vain. Therefore, this book is a call for us to inspect our spiritual foundation today. There are four spiritual foundations discussed in this book: the foundations of spiritual repentance, agreement, forgiveness, and reconciliation. Without spiritual repentance, confession of sin is a meaningless exercise, and the sin remains. Spiritual repentance entails a conscious remorseful pricking of the conscience (repentance within), a 360-degree turn away from all evils, a vow to forsake all evil deeds, and then a confession from a broken heart. The sincere willingness to forsake all evils and obey God's commandments is a sine qua non for true spiritual repentance.

Spiritual agreement entails being one with God—the meeting of the minds as one in agreement. This is the exact relationship that exits between the Father and the Son. As it is written, "I and My Father are one" (Jn 10:30). The simple reason is that the Son is in total agreement with the Father; and as we have read, it is impossible for two individuals to walk together if they are in disagreement. And the key to such spiritual agreement is implicit obedience to the Father. As the Lord said, "And He who sent Me is with Me, the Father has not left Me alone, for I always do those things that please Him" (Jn 8:29).

A house divided can certainly not stand. Those who are born of God have become gods because they are born of God and one with God. For no flesh can worship God in spirit and in truth. But those who are born of God can worship Him in spirit and in truth because they are spirits of God (see Jn 3:6; 1 Cor 2:11–14).

The other two spiritual foundations are presented in conjunction with the first key to the kingdom of God—*love*. As discussed, and appropriately titled, there are two keys to the kingdom of God: *love* and *obedience*. The revelation of these keys is incorporated in the testimony of my conversion, which is part of the introduction of the book. The book discusses, at length, perfect love and implicit obedience as the only keys to the door of eternal life. As gods, those who are born again must, of necessity, possess spiritual attributes such as perfect love or hunger for God and others, which is impossible without implicit obedience. Implicit obedience and doing all things to the glory and pleasure of God is the only greatest spiritual victory. To ensure that our heart is in agreement with God, we must, in all godly sincerity and good conscience, forgive and reconcile with all. There should be a clear difference between the children of God and the unbelievers. We must be as our heavenly Father is (see Mt 5:48). We are gods on earth and the light of God.

The book highlights the blessings of the two keys and ends with a critical question: what else? In that chapter, the Spirit of God pours out some prophetic utterances, which I strongly urge all, especially those who minister to the things of God, to pay particular attention.

My Conversion Testimony

As of the time of this writing, I am still in awe of it all. Those who have known me the longest time still cannot believe it—neither can I. Because not too long ago, about nine or more years ago, I was a fool who thought foolishly that I was a self-made man and my own god. And with many years of flourishing law practice, numerous other successes, and excesses of life, I felt I was my own god. To even imagine that a day would come when I would come full circle with my Maker and Lord would have been considered ludicrous, to say the least. Very recently, a pastor friend in Nigeria reminded me of a letter he wrote to me about twenty-five years ago and what my response was. In the letter, which I considered offensive then, he told me that I had a high calling of God while he was made to assist me. He recounted my response then in which I labeled him the greatest fool to have imagined such thing. The question he puts to me these days is, "who is the fool now?" I never imagined that a day would come when I would teach and defend the Gospel of the kingdom, even for millions of dollars. The last time I spent any significant time reading the Bible was in my high school days; and while it was mandatory, nevertheless, I enjoyed what I considered then as the fiery tales of the Old Testament. I never, in my wildest dream, imagined that what I regarded as foolishness and waste of time, I now strive, by God's grace, to live and teach daily. Now I live and only want to live for God and the work of His kingdom. I now know that God created me primarily for this purpose. And how did it all come about?

It all began about eight thirty in the morning, on the way to my office in the Southwest Houston—about forty-five minutes' drive from my home in Spring, Texas, USA. While driving on Sam Houston Toll Road, at the intersection of the toll way and U.S. Interstate 10, I heard a voice clearly that clearly said, "All your life I have blessed and prospered you, but you have never stopped to give me glory." To say I was completely startled and frightened to my skin would be an understatement. I was quickly flooded with many awful and scary thoughts. To my shock, when I looked behind, there was no one or object on the backseat. I then decided to pull over to the shoulder, and after carefully inspecting the back and the trunk of the car, I nervously drove to my office. About thirty minutes later, I had all my appointments for the day cancelled. I drove back to the house, and there my ordeal began.

As I sat on a couch wondering what had come of me, I heard the same voice again, saying, "I have called you for one purpose only—to go and prepare for the coming of the Lord. The coming of the Lord is at hand. I will send you to the churches to stir them up and get them to examine if they are truly born of God and now ready for the coming of the Lord. I will teach you all you need to know and reveal to you the mysteries of the kingdom of God, but you must live and teach others exactly what I will teach you, lest you will be condemned."

For some inexplicable reason, I summoned the courage to ask why He wanted to send me to His churches. And the response, "Because 99 percent of all those in My churches do not know Me, for how can they know Me when they do not love Me, and how do they love Me when they refuse to obey Me?" From that day, I was confined within my house and environs for three good years while my food was provided by a godsent lady, Deborah Larsen (whom I renamed Queen Raven), a former client, who persisted in seeking me out.

During my in-house confinement, while fasting and praying, I was shown a mighty hand, as white as snow, with two small keys. And I heard the voice say to me, "These are the only keys to the kingdom of God. From the book of Genesis to the book of Revelation, these are the keys given to unlock the kingdom's door. Jesus Christ is the door to the kingdom of God, and the two keys are *love* and *obedience*."

After three years, the Lord opened the doors of some of His churches for me to teach what I was taught in obedience to His instructions. Later I was invited to England; and from there, to the Netherlands; and finally, to Nigeria, which I thought would be for a period of about two months, not knowing I would be ministering intensively in that country for three and half years.

I have taken the time to state my testimony in the hope that it will encourage and strengthen the faith and resolve of fellow believers that our God is truly a living God and that He remains the same, faithful, and merciful forever. It is my fervent prayer that the testimony will minister life to those who are rich in worldly possessions but bankrupt in God; that there is indeed only one needful and imperishable thing—eternal life; and that there is only one whole duty for every person on this earth—love and obey God. For in truth, sooner or later, we shall leave behind all earthly things and return naked as we came.

There is one thing that this book is not, in any manner, intended to accomplish—judgment and condemnation of anyone or group of persons. I therefore appeal to the reader to keep a sincere, open, and renewed mind about the uncompromising truth presented in this book. I am mindful of the unpopularity of the truth of the Gospel of Jesus Christ these days; nevertheless, God is truth, and the truth stands forever and shall judge us in the end. It is my sincerest hope that this book will minister to all of us true repentance and make us return to the love of the truth of the Gospel of Jesus Christ.

Now let us explore the mysteries of the kingdom of God together, and as you read, I pray the Lord grant you His understanding and grace.

The Spiritual Foundations To The Keys

The fundamental problem with most of us Christians is that we have built, and continue to build, our Christian walk and experience on false, wrong, and shaky foundational relationship with God. Worst still, most of us vigorously continue in our belief and reliance on these false foundations, reinforced by denominational doctrines and traditions of men. I am not referring to the various new-member foundation classes, which many churches offer to their new members. While these foundation classes are valuable tools in orienting new members to their new family churches, they hardly, adequately laid the spiritual foundations of true repentance and agreement with God.

The foundations discussed in this book are the fundamental framework in which those who want to seek God with everything they have and those who desire to serve God in spirit and truth must build on. These are the very elect of God who, by the virtue of their election, ought to do as they are given the mysteries of the kingdom of God to understand;

but they are, unfortunately, still building and laboring on false foundations.

As the Lord revealed to me, at least 99 percent of all Christians in all the churches who profess the name of the Lord and Savior, Jesus Christ, do not truly know Him. This, I have discovered, is due to false or shaky foundation in understanding the nature of an intimate spiritual relationship with God.

Without proper understanding of the spiritual foundations to the two keys to the kingdom of God, it is impossible to comprehend and appreciate the mysteries of the two keys, neither for one to truly serve God in spirit and truth. "God is Spirit, and those who worship Him must worship in spirit and in truth" (Jn 4:24). How then can any man worship God in spirit and in truth except when he is the spirit of God; that is, one born of God and led by His Spirit? "For what man knows the things of a man except the spirit of the man which is in him? Even so no one knows the things of God except the Spirit of God" (1 Cor 2:11). Why is it so? "But the natural man does not receive the things of the Spirit of God, for they are foolishness to him; nor can he know them, because they are spiritually discerned" (1 Cor 2:14). What then does it benefit one to spend a lifetime in the church and perhaps professing to be "born again" according to his or her personal conviction, yet at the end of it all, the house falls into a heap of ruin, and he or she is denied entry into the divine rest of Christ?

A popular Christian song in Africa says, "Lord, let me not run this race in vain, that in the end I am not found in your kingdom." And to leave no one in doubt of the nature of this race to the kingdom of God, the scriptures cautioned us, thus: "Not every one who says to Me, 'Lord, Lord,' shall enter the kingdom of heaven, but he who does the will of my Father in heaven. Many will say to Me in that day, 'Lord, Lord,' have we not prophesied in Your name, cast out demons in Your name, and done many wonders in Your name? And then I will declare to them, I never knew you; depart from Me, you who practice lawlessness" (Mt 7:21-23).

Therefore, now is the appointed season for all Christians of all denominations and status to carefully examine and inspect the foundation upon which they are building, or have been building, with a view to ascertaining whether they are building on solid spiritual foundation of truth, righteousness, and holiness—the everlasting foundation. "When the whirlwind passes by, the wicked is no more, but the righteous has an everlasting foundation" (Prv 10:25).

There are four spiritual foundations discussed in this book. The first two foundations, the foundations of spiritual repentance and agreement, are discussed in the first two chapters while the other two, the foundations of spiritual forgiveness and reconciliation, are discussed in chapters 10 thru 12, respectively. Without a clear understanding of these spiritual foundations, the reader may not comprehend and appreciate the mysteries and teachings in this book.

Chapter One

THE FOUNDATION OF SPIRITUAL REPENTANCE

The road to eternal life, as well as any meaningful relationship with God, begins with true repentance. The central message of John the Baptist—as well as the opening message of our Lord and Savior, Jesus Christ, and indeed, other messengers of God—was urging people to repent of their sins. "Repent, for the kingdom of heaven is at hand" (Mt 3:2, 4:17). Spiritual repentance is a complete 360-degree turn away from all evil or sinful ways to God. It is asking God for forgiveness from a broken heart out of good conscience and sincere faith. It is seeking forgiveness from God with all our broken heart and making confession with a mouth that is not in conflict with the heart. God is always looking at our hearts because they are His only true sacrifices. "The sacrifices of God are a broken spirit, a broken and contrite heart—these, O God, You will not despise" (Ps 51:17).

Spiritual repentance involves a torturous conviction, a restless pricking of the spirit, such that gets the spirit in us to mourn for grieving God. The same Spirit of God that

...s us to seek God with all our heart will quicken our abhorrence of sin. If the Spirit of God truly dwells in us, we will experience His immediate conviction when we do wrong. With that, conviction goes to every part of our being. We may find ourselves nervous, anxious, even downright fearful of our own shadow. In this state of uncertainty and guilt, we discover that our prayers no longer go smoothly, and when we try to read the Bible, we fall asleep. There is a feeling of emptiness until we truly repent from the heart and be forgiven; otherwise, we will continue to droop in utter darkness. You will always know when you have been forgiven by God; your heart poured out in mourning for forgiveness and restored of the most important thing you have lost—intimate relationship with God.

This sense of consuming remorse, guilt, and desperation for immediate repentance and restoration is what separates a person born of God from others. The Lord revealed to me that most people who regularly attend churches and profess to know God, even believe they are born again, have their sins not forgiven by God despite their confessions. This is very sad, if not a tragedy. The reason, said the Lord, is that these people confessed their sins with their mouths but repented not in their hearts. Although they made vain confessions with their mouths, there was no spiritual repentance, and therefore, their sins remain. "These people draw near to Me with their mouth, and honor Me with their lips, but their heart is far from Me. And in vain they worship Me, teaching as doctrines the commandments of men" (Mt 15:8-9).

Spiritual repentance requires complete turning away from the offending evils. Let me say it bluntly—it is making a vow to forsake all the evil, sinful ways. God seeks for this penitent heart, which is truly sorry; and the only way to demonstrate

The Foundation Of Spiritual Repentance

remorsefulness is through conscious and sincere decision and willingness not to repeat the wrong. Since true confession follows spiritual repentance, it therefore holds true that without spiritual repentance, confession of sins is void; and the sins remain. Some relevant scriptures will be helpful to the reader:

> If My people, who are called by My name, will humble themselves, and pray and seek My face, and turn from their wicked ways, then I will hear from heaven, and will forgive their sin and heal their land. (2 Chr 7:14)
>
> Let the wicked forsake his way, and the unrighteous man his thoughts; let him return to the Lord, and He will have mercy on him; and to our God, for He will abundantly pardon. (Is 55:7)
>
> Wash yourselves, make yourselves clean; put away the evil of your doings from before My eyes. Cease to do evil, learn to do good; seek justice, rebuke the oppressor; defend the fatherless, plead for the widow. "Come now, and let us reason together," says the Lord, "Though your sins are like scarlet, they shall be as white as snow; though they are red like crimson, they shall be as wool. (Is 1:16-18)
>
> But if a wicked man turns from all his sins which he has committed, keeps all My statues, and does what is lawful and right, he shall surely live; he shall not die. (Ez 18:21)
>
> Repent, and turn from all your transgressions, so that iniquity will not be your ruin. (Ez 18:30)

God alone sees and knows the true hearts of people. He alone knows if a sinner has truly repented, even before he opens his mouth to confess. Therefore, there is no forgiveness from God without spiritual repentance.

The elements of spiritual repentance include, but not limited to, the following:

a. A consuming remorseful acknowledgement of sins—a remorseful conscience which willingly accepts responsibility for sins [like the prodigal son who came to himself] (see Lk 15:17).
b. Repentance within the heart (see Lk 15:18).
c. A vow to forsake, and turn away from all sinful deeds. We must come to God with a determined willingness never to return to the sinful ways (see Lk 15:20).
d. A confession and prayer to God.

The key to spiritual repentance is the resolution or vow or promise to yourself and your God to turn away from those offending ways. Imagine one who confesses the sin of adultery, for example, but he goes out to indulge in the same sin and comes to confess each week. I can say without contradiction that God knew on the first day of the confession that the offender was not serious in mending his ways. Even in our world, a child who disobeys parental rules all the time and each time he says "I am sorry," the parents, no doubt, would not take the child's apology seriously until the child proves that he is truly sorry by forsaking his bad ways. There is a remarkable difference between a first offender and a repeat or habitual offender. "The taste of the pudding is in the eating," the common saying goes. It is not what we say but what we do that matters.

Most of us profess to be born again and new creatures, yet we still remain in bondage of our old evil ways. If such false Christian life persists, the Christian will find himself drifting back totally and completely to the former life, devoid of godly conscience. And that, as the apostle Peter says, is synonymous to a dog returning to its vomit (see 2 Pt 2:1-22). God wants His children to completely forsake and never return to the evil ways they have repented and confessed to Him. To the adulterous woman, the Lord forgave her but admonished her, thus: "Neither do I condemn you; go and sin no more" (Jn 8:11). If that woman left and later turned again to her evil past, then she would not have any excuse. But if she was in the presence of the Lord and she had not resolved not to go back to her sinful ways, then she was never remorseful. It is equally a curse to return to one's evil ways after the knowledge of the truth. To the man who was healed from a thirty-eight-year infirmity, Jesus said, "See, you have been made well. Sin no more, lest a worse thing come upon you" (Jn 5:14). And as the apostle Paul rightly says, if we build again what we have previously destroyed, we become transgressors (see Gal 2:18).

I must confess that I have had many fierce arguments thrown at my face relative to this topic. I fail to understand how anyone who professes to be born of God can justify or rationalize sin—worse still, continue in it. Sin, no matter how we dress it, is a deprivation and abomination to God. There is indeed no other way to put it. There is obviously no middle ground with God. The only way we can demonstrate our fear of God is to depart from evil (sin) and any appearance of evil. The apostle John was very blunt about this: "He who sins is of the devil" (1 Jn 3:8).

These are some of the arguments:

a. *We are flesh and in the world.* That explains it all. If we choose to remain in the world and fulfill the lusts of the flesh, we will never be one with God. If we are true children of God, who are led by His Spirit, we ought not to be of this world; for those who are of the world and in the flesh are not of God and, therefore, need to be born again. The first step toward this spiritual life is the renunciation of sinful, worldly, and fleshly lusts and a total surrender to Jesus Christ. As the scripture says, "For those who live according to the flesh set their minds on the things of the flesh, but those who live according to the Spirit, the things of the Spirit. For to be carnally minded is death, but to be spiritually minded is life and peace. Because the carnal mind is enmity against God; for it is not subject to the law of God, nor indeed can be. So then, those who are in the flesh cannot please God" (Rom 8:5-8).

b. *We are all sinners.* This is certainly true, and for this reason, God sent His only begotten Son to come and show us the way, the truth, and the life. Whoever believes in Jesus and is baptized unto Him is buried in baptism with Him, and as He rose from the dead, we ought to rise with Him, for He has given us the power to become the children of God. The purpose of Jesus was to destroy the works of the devil. Therefore, whoever continues in sin after he has heard or known the truth has no more excuse. "And you know that He was manifested to take away our sins, and in Him there is no sin. Whoever abides in Him does not sin. Whoever sins has neither seen Him, nor known Him" (1 Jn 3:5-6).

c. *God is full of mercy and grace; He will forgive all sins.* Our God is truly merciful, but what is the place of mercy if we continue in sin presumptuously? The apostle Paul correctly stated the point: "And I thank Christ Jesus our Lord who has enabled me, because He counted me faithful, putting me into the ministry. Although I was formerly a blasphemer, a persecutor, and an insolent man; but I obtained mercy because I did it ignorantly in unbelief" (1 Tm 1:12-13). The apostle Paul said he obtained mercy because he acted ignorantly. What does that tell us? If we continue to presumptuously sin because God may forgive us out of the abundance of His mercy, are we then not tempting, mocking, and abusing God's generosity? Again, the apostle Paul, writing concerning grace and sin, asked this all-important question: "What shall we say then? Shall we continue in sin that grace may abound?" (Rom 6:1). In response, he said, "Certainly not! How shall we who died to sin live any longer in it?" (Rom 6:2).

d. *The progression argument.* The argument that is viciously presented to counter the will of God in order to placate people is that turning away from evil/sinful ways involves a progression process. This is the work of the enemy to get us a lazy mind-set. The will of God is that whenever He gives one the grace to understand and know the sinful nature of his deed, he is held accountable if he continues in it. Hence, the Lord warned the adulteress to go and sin no more (see Jn 8:11). For she could no longer avail herself on a claim of ignorance. While it is certainly true that maturity in spiritual walk involves a progression process, God commands us to repent and depart from our evil ways now. Some of us demand for the luxury of gradualism (at our own pace) relative to sin. We want to withdraw from sin in installments, perhaps because we deceive ourselves in believing that we know what tomorrow holds. The sooner we listen to and trust the only one who knows and holds our next breath, the better for us. And by the way, can we claim that we do not know the truth? As it is written, "If I had not come and spoken to them, they would have no sin, but now they have no excuse for their sin" (Jn 15:22). The question now is, what will the Lord say to the Father about us if we continue in sin after we have known the truth? I dare not say, "Father, forgive them for they do not know what they do." That is why the apostle Paul says that there is no remaining sacrifice for those who crucify the Lord afresh with presumptuous sins after knowing the truth (see Heb 6:1-6, 10:26). As the Lord clearly stated, "No one, having put his hand to the plow, and looking back, is fit for the kingdom of God" (Lk 9:62). We have read that in God, there is no occasion of darkness; therefore, those in God can no longer walk in darkness (see 1 Jn 1:5-6, 3:5-10). The one who knows the truth cannot avail himself of his own intentional wrong because he is without excuse (see Rom 1:17-20). Therefore, as it is written, "And everyone who has this hope in Him purifies himself, just as He is pure" (1 Jn 3:3).

THE NATURAL PERSON'S REACTION TO SIN
THE LESSON OF ADAM AND EVE

One striking difference between a true child of God and an unbeliever is their reaction to sin. When a true child of God sins, he is instantly convicted by the Spirit of God in him. He immediately groans in his spirit and heart, and he does not give an excuse, but accepts immediate responsibility, repents, and asks for forgiveness. He does not wait to be reminded. But the unbeliever has little or no conscience, and in any case, he will rather defend himself to the last blood while blaming everyone else.

First Reaction

He attempts to hide in self-denial, thereby deceiving himself. We can hide from others and even succeed in presenting a shiny side, but we certainly can't hide from God (see Jer 23:24). Adam and Eve tried to hide from God (see Gn 3:8-10).

Second Reaction

He attempts to cover the sin from God and others, thereby lying and committing more sins to cover the initial transgression. Adam and Eve covered themselves with leaves (see Gn 3:7). David tried to cover adultery from the eyes of people and, in the process, committed murder (see 2 Sm 12:1-7). Whoever covers his sin shall not prosper. Therefore, let God alone cover our sin—it is a blessing (see Ps 32:1-2). There is no secret with God. (See Prv 28:13; Mt 10:26; Lk 12: 2-3). Covering a sin will lead to greater, more grievous sins, which may ruin the person and even families.

Third Reaction

He declares war against others, thereby blaming everyone else but himself. In other words, the natural person refuses to accept responsibility and show remorse. Adam blamed his wife, Eve (Gn 3:12), and Eve blamed the serpent (Gn 3:13). How so true that this is prevalent in our time.

Fourth Reaction

He declares war against God and blames Him. Adam blamed God for giving him the woman who supposedly got him into trouble (Gn 3:12). Isn't this typical! "It is your fault, God. You made me this way or that way, and that is why I did what I did." Adam and Eve could not have repented and confessed their sins with that kind of heart. Rather, the matter got progressively worse (like every other sin that is not repented of and confessed immediately) from denial to blaming the devil, to blaming others, and finally, to blasphemy. As with progression of sins, there is progression of punishment for transgression—from a lighter rebuke to a more severe punishment if the transgressor refuses to be reformed (see Lv 26). "Woe to him who strives with his Maker" (Is 45:9). The hand of God is lighter on a sinner who spiritually repents immediately when he is convicted by the Holy Spirit, without a reminder from God. If we quickly acknowledge our transgressions, humble ourselves, and repent from a truly broken and contrite heart, the Lord will not cast us away; rather, He will defer His anger for His name's sake.

We will be broken, of course, but the Lord will pick us up, patch the pieces together, and we will live. However, if a sinner waits until God falls on him, he may be ground to powder, and nothing will remain. (See Mt 21:44.) Whoever has ears in his heart to hear, let him hear.

RESTITUTION AND RESTORATION

The topic of restitution/restoration will not be treated elaborately here, but suffice it to say that true spiritual repentance is not complete without restitution. Restitution is a necessary part of repentance. Even in our secular law, whoever seeks equity must do equity, the lack of which may hinder forgiveness. The scriptures are consistent with this position. "If the wicked restores the pledge, gives back what he has stolen, and walks in the statues of life without committing iniquity, he shall surely live; he shall not die" (Ez 33:15). "Then he shall confess the sin which he has committed. He shall make restitution for his trespass in full, plus one-fifth of it, and give it to the one he has wronged" (Nm 5:7).

And again, a reference is made on restitution in the New Testament. When people murmured against Zacchaeus, he said to the Lord, "Look, Lord, I give half of my goods to the poor; and if I have taken anything from any man by false accusation, I restore fourfold" (Lk 19:8). The offender must restore and make whole if he can. Restitution can be both physical and spiritual; and fairly enough, only God knows if you can or cannot physically restore what you have offended. There are certain things or evil deeds that an offender cannot physically restore. Examples that readily come to mind are murder and adultery. In such cases, a true repentance and a vow to forsake (turn away) from such evils and all other evil deeds are necessary. This is spiritual restitution. A classic case of spiritual repentance and restitution involves a case in Texas, where a young man confessed murdering a girlfriend after watching *The Passion of the Christ*. The incident was already ruled as suicide and closed before the later confession. Although I am not in the least position to judge, I can safely say that if that young man is now truly walking with the Lord and continues to do so to the end, his soul will not perish, for he feared not those who might destroy only his body but Him who can kill and also cast anyone into hell. As in his case, in the process of restoration, one may be exposed to reproach and punishment (see 1 Pt 4:12-16). Better that than to fall in the hand of a living God—it is terrible! But to think that one can obtain forgiveness from God while still in possession of that which he took wrongfully is ludicrous, to say the least! God is a just God, respecting for no one but honoring those who honor Him. If the offender can restore but deceives himself with excuses, he brings a curse, not only to himself but also possibly to his family. It is a curse to commingle blood property (blood gain) with one's own. The evil thing will devour the good eventually (see Prv 13:11).

SPIRITUAL REPENTANCE AND PUNISHMENT

Spiritual repentance brings about God's forgiveness, but it does not necessarily waive the punishment relative (in connection) therewith. Forgiveness and punishment are two different things. God has said that every work has its recompense—whether good or bad. As the scripture warns, "Do not be deceived, God is not mocked; for whatever a man sows, that he will also reap" (Gal 6:7). Therefore, God may forgive, but He will not let an offender go unpunished. When the children of Israel sinned against God while they were in the wilderness, Moses pleaded with God to forgive his brethren; God forgave, but He said, "Then the Lord passed by in front of him [Moses] and proclaimed, 'The Lord, the Lord God, merciful and gracious, long-suffering, and abounding in goodness and truth, keeping mercy for thousands, forgiving iniquity and transgression and sin, by no means clearing the guilty, visiting the iniquity of the fathers upon the children and the children's children to the third and fourth generation" (Ex 34:6-7). To leave no one in doubt concerning punishment for every transgression God gave us two examples. In one of the examples, He manifested His reaction to sin, forgiveness, and punishment in the matter of King David's transgression with Bathsheba. David, a man after God's heart, committed murder in an apparent effort to cover his sin of adultery. Later, God, who saw his crime, sent His prophet Nathan to convey His wrath and punishment for the crime. David truly repented, and God forgave him. However, the punishment remained. "Why have you despised the commandment of the Lord, to do evil in His sight? You have killed Uriah the Hittite with the sword; you have taken his wife to be your wife, and have killed him with the sword of the people of Ammon. Now therefore, the sword shall never depart from your house" (2 Sm 12:9-10). And we see that every punishment pronounced against David for that sin came to pass.

Another example is the punishment of King Ahab for dispossessing and murdering Naboth. When the prophet Elijah came from God to Ahab, Ahab humbled himself and truly repented, but the punishment was merely deferred until after his death. Because King Ahab truly humbled himself and repented after he heard God's judgment against him, the Lord sent back Elijah to him, thus: "See how Ahab has humbled himself before Me? Because he has humbled himself before Me, I will not bring the calamity in his days. In the days of his son I will bring the calamity on his house" (1 Kgs 21:29).

In the two examples above, the offenders (King David and King Ahab) tried to cover their sins before men. But can anything be hidden and God not see it? I wonder what would have happened if they were immediately remorseful without a reminder. How about Adam and Eve? Just a thought! Only God knows!

Chapter Two

THE FOUNDATION OF SPIRITUAL AGREEMENT

Every relationship demands for adequate and proper maintenance, and proper maintenance requires proper and honest evaluation and the willpower to do it. A relationship falters and fades away to oblivion when these essential ingredients are lacking. This is more so prevalent with our relationship with God.

As we Christians celebrate and rejoice over our new given (grace) life in Christ Jesus, we sometimes forget to take stock of our relationship with God, whether we are still in agreement with Him. Some, of course, have been celebrating and rejoicing for a course of years, some just a few years, yet others are just beginners. A good number of Christians, especially those who have been there for so long, have now acquired their comfort zone and sometimes their own doctrines and ways. As such, they believe they stand forever. But whether you have been running the race for the kingdom the longest time or you are just beginning, it is of no spiritual consequence. What matters in this race is how well, not how long (see Mt 7:21). Therefore, whoever serves God, not in complete agreement with His will, must lose his race to the kingdom of God. This point was clearly stated by the Lord in the parable of the workers in the vineyard. While some laborers worked for a full-day shift and some only worked for one hour, they received the same amount of wages. God does His things according to His pleasure. He is God, and who can contend with Him?

Therefore as a necessity, it is prudent to take a very honest and proper stock and evaluation of our relationship with God, not once in a while as in secular business but every time and all the time.

We should honestly examine if we have ever been in agreement with God and if we are still in agreement with the original master plan; and if so, are we still now in conformity with that agreement, or have we strayed off course? What if we have never been on course or have strayed off course? What should we do to get back to life? I thank the merciful and gracious God that it is never too late to take the right turn for the race to the kingdom. This is an opportunity to take that right turn, and the hour and day is now! (See Is 55:6; Jn 9:4; 2 Cor 6:2; Heb 3:7-8.) For the life of Christians, every moment we are allowed to live is a borrowed time, and no one knows when the lender will appear to demand for what is rightfully his. It may be as we are now—ready or not, here He comes—or in the middle of the night, like a thief, when sleep is sweetest. As is written, "Watch therefore, for you do not know what hour your Lord is coming" (Mt 24:42). Again, "Therefore you also be ready, the Son of Man is coming at an hour you do not expect" (Mt 24:44). You see, the beloved of God, for a true believer, there is no particular season, for every time is the season to bear fruit and be ready. "Who then is a faithful and wise servant, whom his master made ruler over his household, to give them food in due season? Blessed is that servant whom his master, when he comes, will find so doing. Assuredly, I say to you that he will make him ruler over all his goods" (Mt 24:45-47). Then the Lord went further to pronounce what would happen to that unfaithful servant who was neither ready nor did according to the will of his Lord: "And will cut him in two and appoint him his portion with the hypocrites. There shall be weeping and gnashing of teeth" (Mt 24:51).

THE MYSTERY OF THE CURSED FIG TREE

One of the most striking demonstrations of the life consequence of not walking in total spiritual agreement with God all the time was given to us by the Lord in the Gospel of Mark chapter11. In that chapter, we read the story of the cursed fig tree, to wit:

> As the Lord, Christ Jesus, walked from Bethany, He was hungry, and when He saw the fig tree, He went under it to seek fruit, but found none, and for that He cursed the tree and it withered and died. (Mk 11:12-14)

The mystery of this incident is really in verse 13 of the chapter: "And seeing from afar a fig tree having leaves, He went to see if perhaps He would find something on it. When He came to it, He found nothing but leaves, for it was not the season for figs" (Mk 11:13). Consider this scenario very well. It was not the season for fig trees to bear fruit, yet the Son of the Living God (God Himself) went under it, seeking fruit from it. That does not seem fair, does it? But it is a warning to us that there is no particular season for the children of God, for every time is the season, and when He will come, no one knows. Even the catastrophes all over the world around us are grim reminders of our uncertain and fragile nature—how we may be here today and gone in the next minutes, how those at work cannot return to the house for dinner, etc. Oh, how often do we say it is just happening to others and other places? But is it really?

I pray to the Lord that His Spirit will lead us (Christians) to understand the only motivation and purpose of this book is to get us, especially those who are so hungry and desirous of the truth, to examine ourselves if we are truly walking in spiritual agreement with God and now ready for the coming of the Lord, Jesus Christ. I am not a prophet of doom nor am I aggressive and harsh as some may unfortunately conclude about the truth; but, brothers and sisters in the Lord, God has established His way, the only way to have relationship with Him in spirit and truth, in righteousness and holiness through Jesus Christ our Lord. And we know He is unchangeable, and His way is the right way to eternal life, and that way is a way of righteousness and holiness. I am mindful that these days, what most Christians preach, teach, read, and want to hear are the feel-good messages, prosperity, healing, and miracles because they say it is well with us. I pray that it is well, good, and peaceful with us. But God is God of "if"—if we do what He commands us to do, then it will certainly be well with us. It is a reciprocal relationship. "Say to the righteous that it shall be well with them" (Is 3:10). But in just about most churches, we say peace, peace, when there is no peace (see Jer 6:14). God is with us when we are in spiritual agreement with Him. All we need to do is to return to Him, seek first and all the time the kingdom of God and His righteousness, and we know the rest of the story (see Mt 6:33). Thus says the Lord, "Stand in the ways and see, and ask for the old paths, where the good way is, and walk in it; then you will find rest for your souls. But they said, 'We will not walk in it'" (Jer 6:16).

Frankly, the God of the old, the Lord of Hosts, is still the same God today, doing the same marvelous, wondrous things as He did for the people of old. The problem is that we are not doing what the people of old did, but we want what they had.

Sometime in 2005, I was scheduled to hold a four-day revival for a rather megachurch in Nigeria. Before the program started, the Lord had showed me some dangers many times; nevertheless, He told me to go. The first day of the program was a Thursday, and before I could even say a word, the Lord told me that not even a single soul in that church, including the presiding bishop, had His Spirit. I relayed this message to the bishop and general overseer, and there was groaning. On the third day of the program, being a Saturday, while speaking to the congregation, the Lord commanded me to leave the church and its premises. The time was 8:30 p.m., and that night's program was scheduled to end by 10:30 p.m. I continued speaking for a few minutes, and again, the Lord ordered me to leave. I obeyed and headed to the exit door to the amazement of all. I drove myself to my hotel, not sure what was happening except that I had to obey. At 9:00 p.m. precisely, the entire church and premises were invaded by bloodthirsty armed robbers. The church premises became a battleground between the robbers and the Nigerian Mobile Police. Thank God that no one was seriously hurt or killed though most people in and around the church spent the night in nearby bushes. I was at peace in my hotel room and only found out what happened in the morning. This is just a sampler of the uncountable things that God delivered me from during my three and a half years of evangelism in Africa. Our God indeed knows how to deliver His own, for my eyes have seen His glory. This is not the place to testify of the mind-blowing miracles of the Lord while I was there; suffice it to say that the greatest and most notable was the salvation of souls, the humility and hunger of the people to hear this end-time message of truth and turn away from the faulty foundation and practice and return to the love of the truth. That was the miracle of miracles.

So then, as we celebrate and rejoice over our new given life and of the truth, we ought to celebrate and rejoice; notwithstanding, the exercise is meaningless if we who profess to be buried with Christ in baptism have not yet risen with Him. If we are indeed risen with Christ, we must put on Christ (see Gal 3:27), and be in spiritual agreement with Him, by doing the works He did and walking as He walked (see Jn 14:12; 1 Jn 2:6).

Ironically, some of us think that the great works of Christ were miracles and healings. But in truth, His greatest works were love, obedience, and salvation of souls. We must be Christ on this earth, in total agreement with the Father, the Son, and the Holy Spirit, for the three are one. The million-dollar question is, Christ is risen, but have you truly risen with Him? Every year at Easter, we celebrate the most important event in the life of Christians—the resurrection of our Lord and Savior, Jesus Christ. But in truth, Christ has risen and sits on the right hand of power and majesty, but how many of us today are truly risen with Him? "If then you were raised with Christ, seek those things which are above, where Christ is, sitting at the right hand of God. Set your mind on things above, not on things on the earth" (Col 3:1-2). It is a totally new life based on righteousness and holiness without spots or blemishes—a total fusing together with Christ. "Therefore we were buried with Him through baptism into death, that just as Christ was raised from the dead by the glory of the Father, even so we also should walk in newness of life. For if we have been united together in the likeness of His death, certainly we also shall be in the likeness of His resurrection, Knowing this, that our old man was crucified with Him, that the body of sin might be done away with, that we should no longer be slaves of sin" (Rom 6:4-6). So have you truly risen with Christ?

As we celebrate, it should be a reflective and sober one—a time for stocktaking and careful self-examination of our standing with the Lord. This is why it is spiritually prudent to mourn than to drink and dance away. As the scripture says, "Better to go to the house of mourning than to go to the house of feasting, for that is the end of all men; and the living will take it to heart. Sorrow is better than laughter, for by a sad countenance the heart is made better" (Eccl 7:2-3) (see also Prv 15:13). Furthermore, the Lord proclaimed blessings to those who mourn now from the heart, for they shall be comforted (see Mt 5:4). As apostle Paul said, "For godly sorrow produces repentance leading to salvation" (2 Cor 7:10). Again, the Lord comforted His apostles with these soothing words though difficult to understand. "Most assuredly, I say to you that you will weep and lament, but the world will rejoice; and you will be sorrowful, but your sorrow will be turned into joy" (Jn 16:20). And such joy no one can take it away from us (see Jn 16:22). It is therefore better to mourn now and endure the present sorrow for the eternal joy awaits those who overcome.

That is why we are seriously admonished in the scriptures to be always watchful and careful, lest we get carried away in our self-assured comfort zone, whereby we conclude falsely that we have arrived. "Serve the Lord with fear, and rejoice with trembling" (Ps 2:11). Again, "Therefore, my beloved, as you have always obeyed, not as in my presence only, but now much more in my absence, work out your own salvation with fear and trembling" (Phil 2:12). Is there any more relevant admonition at this time we are in than this? For some reason, some Christians (ministers) have resigned to complacency based on wrong and unbiblical doctrine and belief that once saved, you are saved and will remain saved forever no matter what happens thereafter. What a blatant false belief and doctrine. For why would one work out his own salvation with fear and trembling if he is so sure that from the day he accepted Christ as Lord, his salvation was guaranteed to the end, regardless what he does thereafter. Is it not written, "But he who endures to the end will be saved" (Mt 10:22, 24:13). How then do the first become the last? (See Mt 19:30.)

As we read in the previous chapter, the apostle Paul said that he obtained mercy from God because the evils he did were done out of ignorance. But after we have known the truth, we become bound by it. Are we not privy to the warning that it is impossible to be renewed again if we should fall away after we have known the truth? (See Heb 6:4-6.) And again, whoever puts his hand on the plow and turns back is not fit for the kingdom of God (see Lk 9:62). Isn't the kingdom of God an endurance race? A race is a race to the finish line, and until you get there, you should "work out your own salvation with fear and trembling" (see Phil 2:12). Are not many called but few chosen? Were not all Israelites saved from Egyptian bondage, but how many of them entered the promised land? "But I want to remind you, though you once knew this, that the Lord, having saved the people out of the land of Egypt, afterward destroyed those who did not believe" (Jude 1:5). Assuming, for the purpose of arguments, that the false doctrine is right, how then does one overcome to receive the crown of life, except he endures to the end? (see Rv 2:7, 10, 17, 3:5). And as is written, "But when a righteous man turns away from his righteousness and commits iniquity, and does according to all the abominations that the wicked man does, shall he live? All the righteousness which he has done shall not be remembered; because of the unfaithfulness of which he is guilty and the sin which he has committed, because of them he shall die" (Ez 18:24). It is imperative therefore for every Christian who is truly hungry for the kingdom of God to take this self-examination test, for the day of reckoning is here, and the coming of the Lord is indeed nearer at hand. Let no one deceive and manipulate you with enticing and feel-good words and doctrine. It is only the truth that saves and sets free those who know and pursue it; and the only way to know it is to live it. That was the same reason the Lord cautioned His jubilant disciples who came back in celebrative mood, saying, "Lord, even the demons are subject to us in your name" (Lk 10:17). And the Lord said to them, "Behold, I give you the authority to trample on serpents and scorpions, and over all the power of the enemy, and nothing shall by any means hurt you" (Lk 10:19). What an awesome moment of celebration it had been for these disciples. But the Lord did not spare the truth and reality of the kingdom race as He cautioned them not to celebrate so fast and so much.

"Nevertheless do not rejoice in this, that the spirits are subject to you, but rather rejoice because your names are written in heaven" (Lk 10:20). In other words, it is not what we have accomplished but rather what we have truly become as a result thereof. Therefore, I say to all Christians, rejoice not because Christ is risen but rather rejoice that you have risen with Him. A couple of years back while I was ministering in a church in Africa, the entire church was singing and dancing during offering time; and the words were pleasant, for the congregation was joyfully willing to give. "Offering time!" And the response, "Blessing time!" When I got up to minister, the Lord told me to tell the congregation to remember also that affliction time is a blessing time.

So that our million-dollar question is not forgotten, we will now turn to the next chapter.

Chapter Three

ARE YOU TRULY BORN OF GOD AND RISEN WITH CHRIST?

During one of the days of my in-house confinement, which was referenced in the introduction of the book, the Lord told me that He had called me for one purpose only: to go and prepare people for His coming, and that He would send me to His churches because 99 percent of all those in His churches do not know Him; for how could they know Him when they do not love Him, and how could one love Him except he obeys all He has commanded.

Therefore, every Christian who desires eternal life, no matter the position or length of service in the Lord, should bluntly answer the above question with candor; for whoever deceives himself or herself with the things of the God is doomed forever. For everything written here is specifically according to the teachings the Lord gave me. In the many churches the Lord has led me to minister to, when I asked for a show of hands of all those who believed they were born of God (born again), nearly all hands would be up, but after about ten to fifteen minutes of ministration on the topic and the same question was repeated, hardly any hand would be up. These were people who were honest to themselves, knowing fully well that it was a matter between them and God.

Without a spiritual understanding of what it is to be truly born again, it is not possible to walk in agreement with God. For God is a spirit, and the one who is born of him must, of necessity, be of the spirit. And if of the spirit, it means that one who is born of God is spirit, and if of the Spirit of God, he is god because he is born of God. As thought provoking as this may be, nonetheless, it is biblically true and correct. One who is born of God is a replica of God, fused together in one spirit with God. This is what is meant by total transformation into the image of Christ. This is becoming one with Christ as Christ is one with the Father. "I and My Father are one. He who has seen Me has seen the Father" (Jn 10:30, 14:9). The scriptures tell us that in the beginning, God created man in His image and likeness (see Gen 1:27). That image was a perfect image of God because God is perfect. With the subsequent fall of man went with it the loss of that perfect image. God—out of His loving kindness, grace, and mercy—sent His only begotten Son, Jesus Christ, for the sole purpose of restoring that perfect image and relationship to those who believe and obey His voice. All things produce and reproduce themselves in accordance with their kind; and when God produces or reproduces, He reproduces god. This is being born again as god. It is impossible for a banana tree to produce orange fruits. "But as many as received Him, to them He gave the right to become children of God, to those who believe in His name: 'Who were born, not of blood, nor of the will of the flesh, nor of the will of man, but of God'" (Jn 1:12-13). "That which is born of the flesh is flesh and that which is born of the Spirit

Are You Truly Born Of God And Risen With Christ?

is spirit" (Jn 3:6). In other words, whoever *is* born of God (spirit) is god (spirit).

But how many of us can truly and honestly say that they are one with Christ and therefore gods—the light and salt of the world to unbelievers and even to the devil? Why is this matter of importance? Without a total transformation—i.e., a true Spirit of God—no one can worship God in spirit and in truth. For God is a Spirit, and unless we are spirit of His (born of Him), it is impossible to relate with Him (see 1 Cor 2:11). The natural man (flesh and blood) cannot receive the things of the Spirit of God because they are spiritual, just as flesh and blood cannot enter into the kingdom of God (see 1 Cor 2:14). That is why whoever professes to be in Christ must, of necessity, be a completely new creature without any old raiment of any kind remaining, for when Christ enters, He makes all things new (see Is 65:17; 2 Cor 5:17; Rv 21:5). The problem is that most of us profess to be new, but in reality, we are just clouds without rain because some of the old in us remain to this day. Therefore, most of us are old wine trying to enter into a new bottle. All those in Christ must put on Christ—Christ abides in them, and they abide in Christ. They become Christ, one with Him (see Gal 3:27). They are those led by God's Spirit, and they are the true children of God (see Rom 8:14). And as the scripture says, "But you are not in the flesh but in the Spirit, if indeed the Spirit of God dwells in you. Now if anyone does not have the Spirit of Christ, he is not His" (Rom 8:9).

That is why the scripture relevantly tells us, "He who says he abides in Him ought himself also to walk just as He walked" (1 Jn 2:6). Therefore, those who are born of God must work in newness of life anchored on righteousness and holiness as God is. "And that you put on the new man who was created according to God, in true righteousness and holiness" (Eph 4:24). I recommend that the reader endeavors to read Ephesians 4, especially verses 14-32. These verses give a glimpse of an insight of the new creature in Christ.

Being mindful of a chance that some readers might be uneasy with the position and statement that whoever is born of God is god, let the scriptures be the source. In the book of Psalms, God called His true children gods: "I said, 'You are gods, and all of you are children of the Most High'" (Ps 82:6). Our Lord cited this scripture to the Jews who were offended by His claim that He was one with the Father. "Is it not written in your law, 'I said, You are gods'?" (Jn 10:34). Assuring Moses of the power and authority of the new spirit in him, God made him understand that he (Moses) was god to others. Concerning the ministerial relationship between Moses and Aaron, God said: "So he shall be your spokesman to the people. And he himself shall be as a mouth for you, and you shall be to him as God" (Ex 4:16). And concerning Pharaoh, God said to Moses, "See, I have made you as God to Pharaoh" (Ex 7:1). When we are in agreement with God, His Spirit abides in us, and as such, we become gods to unbelievers, and even demons.

Chapter Four

THE SPIRITUAL CHARACTERISTICS OF BORN OF GOD

Briefly stated and explained herein are the four key characteristics of a person born of God. These are the key godlike attributes, and if any Christian lacks any of them, the individual is yet to be born again. As explained earlier, one who is born of the Spirit (God) is spirit (god). It goes without saying then that one who is a spirit must, of necessity, be adored with spiritual characteristics and attributes. I realize that each of these four characteristics can take a life of its own as a full separate chapter in a book. However, for the purpose of this book and for the call for self-examination, they are discussed here briefly and to the point. In the many churches where the Lord had led me to minister, I had tried to emphasize the essential place of these attributes in the life of a born of God by suggesting that Christians write and place them in a strategically conspicuous corner of the house, where they may read and ask themselves questions daily. It can be one of the most effective daily devotional readings. Being born of God is being god on earth, living all the time to please Him, in conforming and agreeing with Him, living and being the truth. Therefore, as spirits, we must have a spiritual heart, a spiritual mind, a spiritual body, and a new spirit.

SPIRITUAL HEART

If we are truly born of God, we must indeed have a new heart: a heart of perfect love, compassion, mercy, forgiveness, humility, submission, and obedience to all the words, commandments, and doctrines of Christ. This is a broken and contrite heart, which God swore He would not despise, because such heart is God's heart and His only acceptable sacrifice. "The sacrifices of God are a broken spirit, a broken and a contrite heart—these, O God, You will not despise" (Ps 51:17). This new heart is given by God to those who are truly willing to totally surrender to His will; for without a spiritual heart, no person can love and obey God as God commands us to and talk less of loving our enemies. "Cast away from you all the transgressions which you have committed, and get yourselves a new heart and a new spirit" (Ez 18:31). And again, "Then I will give them one heart, and I will put a new spirit within them, and take the stony heart out of their flesh, and give them a heart of flesh" (Ez 11:19). "For this is the covenant that I will make with the house of Israel after those days, says the Lord. I will put my laws in their mind and write them on their hearts, and I will be their God, and they shall be My people" (Heb 8:10). For those who are the elect of God, and born of Him, is fulfilled in them this promise of a new covenant relationship with God, whereby God lives in them. This is a total transformation into His image; it is being born again of God.

And for what reason does God give us a new heart? So that, first, we can obey His commandments. "That they may walk in My statutes and keep My judgments and do them; and they shall be My people, and I will be their God" (Ez 11:20). Second, our heart must be pure, for God dwells there, and He is holy and dwells in holy places, and only those who are pure in heart shall see Him: "Blessed are the pure in heart, for they shall see God" (Mt 5:8). A new creature must, of necessity, have a new heart. The scriptures state that when the Spirit of God came upon King Saul, he became another man with a new heart. "So it was, when he had turned his back to go from Samuel, that God gave him another heart" (1 Sm 10:9). The danger for most of us is that we are like snakes, which shed the old skins for new ones but still retain the old venomous hearts. As says the scripture, "For he is not a Jew who is one outwardly, nor is circumcision that which is outward in the flesh; but he is a Jew who is one inwardly; and circumcision is that of the heart, in the spirit" (Rom 2:28-29).

SPIRITUAL MIND

One born of God must have a spiritual mind that is renewed all the time, a mind raised with Christ and set on things that are above where Christ sits on the right hand of Majesty. That is why the scriptures strongly urge the true born of God to be renewed in the spirit of their minds so as not to walk in futility as unbelievers. "This I say, therefore, and testify in the Lord, that you should no longer walk as the rest of the Gentiles walk, in the futility of their mind. And be renewed in the Spirit of your mind" (Eph 4:17, 23). The preceding scripture clearly shows that there is a spiritual mind that needs to be renewed all the time in the life of one who is born of God. For one who is born of God is a spirit and has the mind of Christ, and the mind of Christ is spiritual (see 1 Cor 2:16).

It is an obvious truth that our greatest battles are waged in the mind, and it is equally obvious that whatever controls our mind process controls us. Therefore it is absolutely imperative for a true born again / born of God to win the battle of the mind. It is indeed impossible to fight a spiritual battle with a carnal mind. "For though we walk in the flesh, we do not war according to the flesh. For the weapons of our warfare are not carnal but mighty in God for pulling down of strongholds" (2 Cor 10:3-4). The apostle Paul, in the same chapter, explained to us how we can successfully fight this spiritual war: "Casting down imaginations, and every high thing that exalteth itself against the knowledge of God, and bringing into captivity every thought to the obedience of Christ" (Authorized [King James] Version, 2 Cor 10:5).

Just returning from over three years of evangelism work in Nigeria and as it is with most developing nations of the world, I must, without contradiction, say that the greatest hindrance to spiritual growth and maturity of Christians in these parts is the bondage of spiritual fear of the unknown. Sadly enough, the ever-domineering fear of the powers of darkness, wickedness, and evil forces have so paralyzed the light that these nations are plunged into horrible darkness never known before. Yet despite the proliferation of churches on every corner, these nations seem to wallop in cyclical saga of perpetual bondage of spiritual fear of the unknown. Even at worst, spiritual fear has taken a center stage of ungodly commercialism being fueled and reinforced by the very institution (church), which was originally commissioned to help set the captives free. It is abominable that the very ministers of the

Gospel, who have been entrusted to encourage, strengthen, and feed the flock, are now agents of spiritual bondage—the devourer and destroyer of God's vineyard (see Jer 12:10, 23:2, 11; Ez 34:1-6; Mt 23:14; 1 Tm 4:1-2; 1 Pt 2:1-6). Driven by covetousness, they have succeeded in getting just about everyone to believe in the devil. Everyone is possessed with or has some evil forces chasing him or her, every beautiful young woman has a marine spiritual husband, every misfortune is a result of evil person who has tied the fortune. Some lizards are monitoring spirits; the cat is demonic. Every barrenness is due to witchcraft; every miscarriage is caused by an evil person who has stolen the fetus from the womb. Special prayers are conducted in bushes (bush prayer), on riverbanks, washing the body with the blood of unblemished lamb, with animal sacrifices orchestrated and conducted by these agents of darkness parading themselves as ministers of Christ, etc. Now where do I begin and stop to tell of these abominable and ungodly teachings and practices, which have brought almost total spiritual blindness to these nations more than it has ever been? And what with all the enticing, crafty, manipulative, deceptive, and lying devices? They get people to accept spiritual bondage while they make merchandise of them, devouring and charging huge sums of money for the so-called special, deliverance, and liberation prayers. And this they do without conscience while they say, "Peace, peace," when there is no peace. As written in the book of Jeremiah, "Because from the least of them even to the greatest of them, everyone is given to covetousness; and from the prophet even to the priest, everyone deals falsely. 'They have also healed the hurt of My people slightly, saying, "peace, peace!" when there is no peace. Were they ashamed when they had committed abomination? No! They were not at all ashamed; nor did they know how to blush. Therefore they shall fall among those who fall; at the time I punish them, they shall be cast down,' says the Lord" (Jer 6:13-15). The Lord abhorred similar practices of the Pharisees, thus: "Woe to you, Scribes and Pharisees, hypocrites! For you devour widows' houses, and for pretence make long prayers. Therefore you will receive greater damnation" (Mt 23:14). As the Lord abhorred and severely punished the house of Eli over the abuse of His sacrifice (a vulnerable broken heart), so shall it be with this generation of deceivers, manipulators and liars who prey on the weak and the most vulnerable children of God (see 1 Sm 2:22-26, 27-36). Then, the Lord said to Samuel, "Behold, I will do something in Israel at which both ears of everyone who hears it will tingle. In that day I will perform against Eli all that I have spoken concerning his house, from beginning to end. For I have told him that I will judge his house forever for the iniquity which he knows, because his sons made themselves vile, and he did not restrain them. And therefore I have sworn to the house of Eli that the iniquity of Eli's house shall not be atoned for by sacrifice or offering forever" (1 Sm 3:11-14). And what did the sons of Eli do that provoked such wrath of God? They abused God's best sacrifice; the greatest sacrifice of God is a broken heart, which is desperately seeking for Him. They took improper advantage of vulnerable women who came to seek the Lord (see 1 Sm 2:22). The abuse of such sacrifice under the color of authority of priesthood or calling, or in the name of the Lord, is abomination of an epic proportion in the sight of God. Undoubtedly, God set the Eli example for all who profess to be servants of the living God. My prayer is for the Lord to use this piece to bring total repentance and turn around in all His churches.

    I am not denying the obvious fact that wickedness and evil powers lurk around every corner of our world as I was, in no small measure, a victim of such horrible wicked acts. I admit

The Spiritual Characteristics Of Born Of God

there may be witches (real and imagined) in just about every nation. Therefore, let me dispel the condemnation of some who might accuse me of naiveté of the dangerous situations prevalent in those societies. Notwithstanding, I am speaking concerning the church of Jesus Christ and, more specifically, to those who claim to be born again but still old in their minds and beliefs.

One who is spiritually fearful is still in darkness, not knowing his or her way. For if while we are in the world, we are not the light of the world, we are certainly in darkness. "This is the message which we have heard from Him and declare to you, that God is light and in Him is no darkness at all. If we say that we have fellowship with Him, and walk in darkness, we lie and do not practice the truth" (1 Jn 1:5-6). The one who is spiritually fearful of the unknown is in bondage; he does not have freedom or liberty. For he is not yet delivered from the domain of darkness and cannot serve God without fear (Col 1:13; Lk 1: 74-75). "Now the Lord is the Spirit; and where the Spirit of the Lord is, there is liberty" (2 Cor 3:17). What does this tell us? Simply, where there is no Spirit of God, there can never be freedom and liberty. It then holds true that whoever is spiritually fearful does not have the Spirit of God in him and is not a new creature, for one cannot be new and old at the same time. Therefore, he is not born of God (born again). For in reality, those who are born again are all new creatures who have been delivered from the domain of darkness and transformed into the image of Christ so that they can serve God in righteousness and holiness all the days of their life without fear. It goes without saying then that a Christian who is still spiritually fearful of the unknown is not only in bondage still but declaring that there are greater in the world than the one in him. For a truth, we fear those forces that are greater and more powerful than us. And whoever is afraid has already lost the battle before it even started. For he is spiritually blind and cannot see that those who are with him are more than those who are against him (see 2 Kgs 6:16-17).

In churches and prayer gatherings in Africa and most other developing parts of the world, the most joyful and exciting time during services would be the general recitals of the wonderful promises of God's deliverance and protection like: "No weapon formed against you shall prosper" (Is 54:17). But that is where it ends—a mere recital. If one claims that God—the Almighty God, the Alpha and Omega, the Lord of Hosts—is truly with him and still remains in spiritual bondage of fear, he is a liar. Besides, one who is spiritually fearful has no spiritual power and no good and sound mind. "For God has not given us a spirit of fear, but of power and of love and of a sound mind" (2 Tm 1:7).

Again, the death and resurrection of Jesus Christ is in vain for a Christian who is enslaved by the bondage of fear of death, since Christ came to overcome death for us. "And release them who through fear of death were all their lifetime subject to bondage" (Heb 2:15).

When I would ask the congregations what they were afraid of, their only answer reflected how misunderstood the status of a Christian as a (god) born of God was. The only culprit for fear is *death*. And when I responded and told them that I had divine good news, their eyes would pop up in anxiety, excitement, and anticipation. The good divine news is, "We shall all die, so let not fear kill us physically before our time." For if we truly believe that all those who are in Christ—born of God—have died and risen with Him, what shall we say of those who profess Him and still are fearful of death? "Most assuredly, I say to you, he who hears My word and believes in Him who sent Me has everlasting life, and shall not come into judgment, but has passed from death into life" (Jn 5:24).

On the way to a revival program, the Lord asked me to tell the congregation to raise for Him "a generation of gods, a generation free from bondage of the mind." Further, the Lord told me that most Christians, if not all Christians, in these developing countries believe in the devil and are like the big rooster (cock) that runs away terrified at the slightest approach or imagination of the appearance of a kite. And when I shared these revelations to the congregations, there was indignation before they finally understood. You see, whoever we believe in his works so much so that he influences us thereby, especially when such works make us to fear and dismay, we spiritually believe in him. Therefore, if we say we do not believe in the devil but we believe in his works so much that such belief influences and controls our mind considerably, we still believe in the devil; for the devil and his works are the same. When the apostle Philip asked the Lord to show them the Father, the Lord answered among other things, "Believe Me that I am in the Father and the Father in Me, or else believe Me for the sake of the works themselves" (Jn 14:11).

As for the rooster illustration, it is better understood by people who were raised or are living in rural areas, more commonly villages. Without fail, and rather very early in the morning, the cock asserts its authority as the king of the birds with his wings and loud crows. But no sooner, a small kite appears or is imagined to appear in the air above, the big cock runs for dear life, gripped with fear of death. You see, the cock has grown beyond the ability of a kite to carry it, but still the cock is blinded by the bondage of fear, and for that, it will never be free or at liberty. Like the rooster, which acquired its fear from mama hen, our spiritual fear is neither hereditary nor real. But it was passed from generation to generation. This explains why the children who are born and raised here in the United States and Europe are not saddled with such crushing bondage. The greatest danger is that the very institution, which is the only hope of spiritual freedom and liberty, is now at the helm of exploitation, manipulation, deceit, and lies.

As I said earlier, I know what it means to suffer in the hands of the wicked and devilish forces, but I believe in the power and authority of Jesus Christ as greater than all the forces in this world. I believe from the heart the word of God that if He is with me, nothing can stand before me. Besides, we cannot overcome and cast out the enemy (demon) when we are afraid of him. The greatest tactic of the devil is fear, and God knows this so very well that in all situations when He appeared to His people the first two words He spoke were *fear not*. The book of Joshua reveals a lot. God told Joshua to be strong and of good courage so that he might obey Him implicitly. He also commanded Joshua not to fear because He would be with him wherever he went (see Jo 1:9). Further, God promised Joshua what He has promised to us: "No man shall be able to stand before you all the days of your life" (Jo 1:5). These two verses quoted above are the favorite of most churches because they are encouragement boosters, but hollow ones at best until we adhere to God's words and commandment as Joshua did. "This book of the law shall not depart from your mouth, but you shall meditate in it day and night, that you may observe to do according to all that is written in it. For then you will make your way prosperous, and then you will have good success" (Jo 1:8).

Could it then be that the paralyzing spiritual bondage of fear among those who profess to be born again in these countries is due to lack of perfect love and implicit obedience to the word of God? The scriptures tell us that whoever is afraid (spiritually) is not perfect in love because perfect love eliminates fear, and God is love (see 1 Jn 4:16, 18). So whoever is not perfect in love is not perfect in God. I conclude therefore that anyone who has spiritual fear of the unknown is yet to be born of God.

SPIRITUAL BODY

Our mortal body, crucified and buried in baptism with Christ, becomes new and transformed into a spiritual temple where God dwells. That which is new is new for any and all purposes. And where there remains a shade of the old in that which is said to be new, it certainly is not new. This is the case with most of us who profess to be born again. Whatever our body (flesh) lusts after controls us, and whoever we employ our body to serve is indeed our true master. "Do you not know that to whom you present yourselves slaves to obey, you are that one's slaves whom you obey, whether of sin leading to death or of obedience leading to righteousness?" (Rom 6:16). Our Lord and Savior, Jesus Christ, said it plainly to us that in this world, there are two contending powers over our being, and the one we obey/yield to is the one we love; and we cannot serve two masters (see Mt 6:24). Therefore, what we do with our bodies clearly shows if we are of and for God or against Him. The one who is born of God ought not to defile God's dwelling place. "He who sins is of the devil, for the devil has sinned from the beginning. For this propose the Son of God was manifested, that He might destroy the works of the devil" (1 Jn 3:8).

Now, this may sound harsh to some of us, but it is the single truth. If a child of God would, for a moment, have a deeper comprehension what it means that God dwells in him and that he is the true house of God, then he can appreciate why his body should be the holiest temple ever. The spiritual body of one born of God must be holier than any temple/church built with hands. Thus says the Lord, "'Heaven is My throne, and earth is My footstool. Where is the house that you will build Me? And where is the place of My rest? For all those things My hand has made, and all those things exist,' says the Lord. 'But on this one will I look: on him who is poor and of a contrite spirit, and trembles at My word'" (Is 66:1-2). Knowing then that God's true dwelling place is our body, those who are truly of Him ought to sanctify themselves in purity, righteousness, and holiness all the days of their lives by crucifying and mortifying the flesh and bringing it subject and obedient to the Spirit of God (see Rom 6:6; 2 Cor 10:5; Gal 5:24; Eph 4:24; 1 Jn 3:3). Except this is so, one can never be truly born of God. But in truth, most professing born-again Christians have driven God out of His house and turning that which should be the holiest temple into the house of merchandise and the devil. Sadly, most of us, by our actions, defile more than just the temple of God within us, thereby dragging others along to a destructive path.

The scriptures tell us that for the first time in the life of our Lord, Jesus Christ, He expressed open anger and hostility against those who were defiling the temple of God, which temple was built by hand. Now imagine what He would do to the one who defiles His true dwelling place. Thank God for not leaving us in doubt. "Do you not know that you are the temple of God, and that the Spirit of God dwells in you? If anyone defiles the temple of God, God will destroy him. For the temple of God is holy, which temple you are" (1 Cor 3:16-17). Even now, behold, He stands by the door of His house, would you let Him in forever? If you love God and keep His house clean, you will be blessed forever; for then you can proudly say, "The kingdom of God is within *me*."

NEW SPIRIT

A born of God must have a new spirit—the Spirit of God replacing the spirit of man. With this spirit, one can easily, and without thought, love and serve God in truth and spirit. Without this new spirit, it is impossible to obey God implicitly. It is only this new spirit that enables us to love others even as God loves us and even love our enemies and do all these things that are impossible for the flesh to do. When the enabling Spirit of God dwells in us, nothing shall be impossible. "For with God nothing will be impossible" (Lk 1:37). This is the Spirit of God, and whoever does not have this new spirit is none of His (see Rom 8:9). Without a new spirit, one cannot do the works of Christ and be Christ on earth; therefore, without this new spirit, we can do nothing. "Then I will give them one heart, and I will put a new spirit within them" (Ez 11:19).

And why does God give us this new spirit? "That they may walk in My statues, and keep my judgments and do them" (Ez 11:20). Therefore, without this new spirit, no man can understand the mysteries of God. This is the spirit that quickens one to be divinely humble, meek, and long-suffering. The same spirit gets you to thank God from the heart for any and all things. The new spirit gives you the spiritual attitude to take afflictions and tribulations as blessings and as opportunity to overcome the evil ones and glorify the name of the Lord. If only we can understand that all we need do is to seek God with a total surrender and uncompromising willingness to obey and that God Himself will give us the enabling spirit to do the impossible, we will never have to consider God's commandments as burdensome.

One typical example of a test of this new spirit can be found in the Gospel of Luke 9. As the Lord journeyed toward Jerusalem, He sent two of His apostles, John and James, to a Samaritan village to make ready for Him, but the people of the village refused Him. The two brothers (John and James) were so offended at the slight that they reacted angrily and asked, "Lord, do you want us to command fire to come down from heaven and consume them, just as Elijah did?" (Lk 9:54). And the Lord's reaction was swift. He turned and rebuked them and said, "You do not know what manner of Spirit you are of" (Lk 9:55). Most Christians today still do not understand the new spirit they are of, and as such, they lack this all-important attribute of one born of God. For in truth, no man is capable of loving his enemies unless he is truly born of this new Spirit.

Chapter Five

WE ARE WHAT WE DO, NOT WHAT WE SAY

It is of spiritual necessity for those who are born of God to have the four characteristics/attributes enshrined in them because they are what they do and not just what they say. While it is hard for one to speak bad about himself, what he does bear correct witness of who he is. A thief is a thief because he steals. If those who profess to be born of God walk, talk, and act as unbelievers, they are unbelievers. For it is not what we say but what we do that bears witness that we are the children of God and true disciples of Jesus Christ. When the Jews of Christ's days asked Him to tell them plainly if He was the Christ Jesus, He answered and said to them, "I told you, and you do not believe. The works that I do in My Father's name, they bear witness of Me" (Jn 10:25). So whatever we do and how we do it bears witness that we are of God or of the devil. If we do the good works of God, we are of God, and people will behold (without a word) the good works and will conclude that we are of God. "Let your light so shine before men, that they may see your good works and glorify your Father in heaven" (Mt 5:16). "Having your conduct honorable among the Gentiles, that when they speak against you as evildoers, they may, by your good works which they observe, glorify God in the day of visitation" (1 Pt 2:12). It is true then that whatever we do that does not please God glorifies the devil, and whoever glorifies the devil is of the devil (see 1 Jn 3:8).

Responding to the Jews who boasted of Abraham as their father, our Lord said to them, "If you were Abraham's children, you would do the works of Abraham" (Jn 8:39). As the scripture says, "Therefore by their fruits you will know them" (Mt 7:20). In other words, if I observe what you do, I can say who you are. For what we do speaks louder than what we say, and our action betrays our hidden motive.

While I was ministering in Africa, I was shown a table with two men sitting on it. I was told that one of the men professed to be born again and the other was a child of the devil. Then I was instructed to identify which of the two was the child of God. Sadly, I couldn't distinguish between the two. While they were wearing different uniforms outwardly, I was shown that their hearts were similarly full of darkness. The man who professed to be born again was like a snake that has shaded off the old skin for a new one but is still a venomous snake at heart. That was a sobering and painful experience for me, and I wept. God sees the heart, and no matter what we profess to be or think, God only knows the heart. For such hypocrisy, the Lord pronounced woes to the Pharisees and scribes, comparing them to a cup that is clean outside but full of dirt inside; and very freshly painted graves that appear beautiful outwardly but inside are full of dead bones and other filthy things (see Mt 23:25-27). As it was with the Pharisees and scribes of the old, so it is today with most Christians. Hence, this admonishment from the Lord: "For I say to you, that unless your righteousness exceeds the righteousness of the scribes and Pharisees, you will by no means enter the kingdom of heaven" (Mt 5:20).

One who is born of God is born of God inwardly, and that which is inwardly is manifested outwardly by what we do, not just what we say alone (see Rom 2:29). Therefore, as the Lord instructed me to warn a congregation, "Seek not to look good, but be good." Not living what we teach or preach is outright hypocritical and self-righteous, having no restraint in judging and condemning others while we ourselves commit abominations (see Rom 2:17-24).

We see then that for us to walk together with God, we must walk in complete agreement, and we cannot do so except when we are born of Him; and being born of Him, we take on His image and become gods. And since God is light, everything of, about, and in Him ought to be light. Therefore there should not be any occasion of darkness in those who are born of God (see 1 Jn 1:5-7). This is the only foundation on which we must strive to build on, and it is the only imperishable goal for those who desire the kingdom of God. "But if we walk in the light as He is in the light, we have fellowship one with another" (1 Jn 1:7). It is neither about just leaving one church or denominational doctrine for another, nor is it about seeking for places to feel good or see miracles, rather, it is about becoming one with God—inseparable. It is about an indescribable fusing together in relationship with God—a relationship anchored on spiritual hunger for God and implicit obedience to His words and commandments. I can hear some people asking the appropriate question of who can do this since we are humans and God is God. Can any man be holy? The question is genuinely to the point. And the answer is no. No one can be in agreement with God and holy except when he is born again of God. This is the truth of the word of God, for He commanded us to be holy and perfect as He is. A Christian should accept the pronouncement of God without question. And if we ask any question, it should be how we do the will of God, not why should God require this or that of us. This is living by faith. The scripture says that "the just shall live by faith" (Rom 1:17). For it is written, "But without faith it is impossible to please Him, for he who comes to God must believe that He is, and that He is a rewarder of those who diligently seek Him" (Heb 11:6). Perhaps that explains the problem with many of us Christians. We are neither just nor seriously willing and striving at all cost to be just and holy. Therefore, we are unable to live by faith. Instead of forsaking the sinful ways, the moment we hear the truth, we rather resort to excuses. As God revealed to me that 99 percent of the people in all the churches where His name is called do not know Him, it goes without contradiction that perhaps 99 percent of all those professing to be Christians do not understand what it really means to be born of God—just as Nicodemus, the great Pharisee, could not comprehend it. Nicodemus may be excused, for he was not privy to the teachings of Jesus Christ before the night encounter with Him. But what excuse do we have to give today? As the Lord said, "If had not come and spoken to them, they would have no sin, but now they have no excuse for their sin" (Jn 15:22). And again, it is written, "For the wrath of God is revealed from heaven against all ungodliness and unrighteousness of men, who suppress the truth in unrighteousness, because what may be known of God is manifest in them, for God has showed it to them. For since the creation of the world His invisible attributes are clearly seen, being understood by the things that are made, even His eternal power and Godhead, so that they are without excuse" (Rom 1:18-20). God sent His only begotten Son to come and show the only way to His kingdom; we will never expect any other greater authority than Jesus Christ. As is written: "God, who at various times and in various ways spoke in time past to the fathers by the prophets, has in these last days spoken to us by His Son, whom He has appointed heir of all things, through whom He made the worlds" (Heb 1:1-2).

Sin, no matter how we dress it, is sin; and a deprivation, an offense to God. And except when one is in the spirit, walking in the spirit, he cannot understand the spiritual things and mysteries of God, for they are spiritual. One may read the Bible every day for one hundred years and still not know or understand the words therein, except when they are revealed to him by the same Holy Spirit who inspired the scriptures. We know that with God, all things are possible to those who believe and do His will.

The spiritual foundations we have just discussed are absolutely necessary to understand ourselves in the Lord and the mysteries of the two keys to the kingdom of God, which are discussed in the next chapters. It is my fervent prayer that the Spirit of God that inspired this end-time message and the writing of this book will bring you to the understanding of the hour we are in, transform you into His true image, and motivate you to make an everlasting vow to return today (now) to the love of the truth, which is the first love, into a glorious reunion with your God and Father through Jesus Christ, our Lord and Savior. To Him be all the glory and dominion forever. Amen.

Prelude To The Two Keys

On one of those blessed days of my confinement in the house, which was alluded to in the introduction of this book, while fasting and praying, I was shown a mighty hand as white as snow with two small keys. A voice said to me, "These are the only keys to the kingdom of God. From the book of Genesis to the book of Revelation, there are no other keys given to the kingdom of God. Jesus is the only door to the kingdom of God, and the only two keys to that door are *love* and *obedience*."

The Gospel of the kingdom of God is about relationship with God and fellow human beings. God is embodied in these two most important keys. Without proper and spiritual understanding and living of these all-important keys, one cannot enter into God's rest. It is on these two keys that the kingdom of God is anchored on, and they are the specific keys the Lord came down from heaven to establish here on earth. For that reason, therefore, all those who are truly of Jesus Christ have the kingdom of God within them by the knowledge of the truth, which is the perfection of these two keys in them. To know these two keys is to know God: the only way to know the two keys is to live them, the only way to live God is to love Him, and the only way to love Him is to obey Him.

These two keys are the cornerstone of all the commandments of God. When asked which was the greatest commandment, the Lord answered that the first and greatest commandment is to love God with everything we have; and the second, which is like the first, is to love others as we love ourselves (see Mt 22:37-39). Then, he concluded, thus: "On these two commandments hang all the Law and the Prophets" (Mt 22:40). The first and the second great commandments are intertwined and interdependent, for one cannot exist without the other, for love cannot be effectuated without implicit obedience. The fault with many of us is the false foundation, belief, and practice of separating love and obedience, whereby we erroneously think that we can love God devoid of implicit obedience. The only way to truly love, submit, thank, and honor God is to obey Him. "If you love Me, keep My commandments. If anyone loves Me, he will keep My word; and My Father will love him, and We will come to him and make Our home with him" (Jn 14:15, 23).

One striking problem is that most of us consider that our desire to please God is sufficient and independent of the love for others. This amounts to false living; for if we do not love others as God loves us, we are not of Him and do not truly love God (for God is perfect love). "A new commandment I give to you, that you love one another; as I have loved you, that you also love one another. By this all will know that you are My disciples, if you have love for one another" (Jn 13: 34-35). With Christ, the barometer of love is raised to a much higher level. Those who are born of God are commanded to love as God because they are gods. They must be perfect in love as

God is (see Mt 5:48). That is why we are commanded to love our enemies and bless those who curse us. We know that on our own, we are incapable of perfect love, but God, who cannot lie, has given those who are born of Him the enabling spirit to do that which is humanly impossible. "But he who hates his brother is in darkness and walks in darkness, and does not know where he is going, because the darkness has blinded his eyes" (1 Jn 2:11). The greatest difficulty or problem of being a truly born of God hinges on these two keys. Any Christian who accepts and spiritually understands and lives these two keys (the keys of life) shall see God at the end. At the same token, anyone who lacks these keys, or any one of them, or keeps them not in complete accordance with the will of God is laboring in vain (see Mt 7:21-23). I hereby employ you in the name of the Lord to give every detailed attention today to these two keys, with a view to living them to perfection; and I pray the Lord to grant you the divine understanding of the mysteries of these two keys as we now proceed to discuss them.

LOVE:
THE FIRST KEY TO
THE KINGDOM OF GOD

Chapter Six

THE SPIRITUAL HUNGER FOR GOD

One horrible misconception and false belief among us is that we love God enough by going to church regularly and doing the little we do. This is always a pitfall, giving most Christians false sense of comfort zone and security. However, there is a level of intensity of love of God that is expected from us in our relationship with Him as His children—the intensity of love that drives a true child of God *crazy* about God and things of God. No one can attain this level except through the presence of the Spirit of God. This is a love relationship with God where nothing else comes second to Him, much less before Him, in the affairs of life. It is a spiritual hunger for God that passes all understanding. It is such an overwhelming hunger that gets God's attention and makes Him not pass over His own. Unfortunately, most Christians neither have nor understand this spiritual hunger; rather, they assume wrongly that they have enough love for God until they are confronted with a test or trial.

FORSAKING ALL FOR THE LOVE OF GOD

One of the greatest tests of our love of God is the willingness to give it all up (including that which we consider to be the most important thing to us) for the kingdom. How far are we willing to go? We say we love God with all our hearts but wait until we are tested or afflicted. Blessed is he who does not offend God at the breaking point of trial or affliction. This point was clearly exemplified in the Gospel of Matthew 19, in the story of the rich young ruler. As the story goes, a certain rich young man came to Jesus and asked Him what good he could do in order to enter into the kingdom of God (see Mt 19:16). Jesus told him to keep God's commandments if he desired eternal life (verse 17). And the rich young man sought to know which commandments he should keep. And the Lord answered by citing some of the commandments while leaving out the most important commandment—love (verses 18, 19). Now, hear the rich young man, "All these things I have kept from my youth. What do I still lack?" (Mt 19:20). That sounds like most of us; we assume we are complete in our love of God above everything, yet when tested, we fall flat on our faces and short of the most important commandment: "You shall love the Lord your God with all your heart, with all your soul, and with all your strength" (Dt 6:5).

In response to his boastful question, the Lord threw in a test of love of God. "If you want to be perfect, go, sell what you have and give to the poor, and you will have treasure in heaven; and come, follow me" (Mt 19:21). Of course, we know the reaction of the rich young man—indignation and unwillingness to part with his worldly possession for the love of God (verse 22). There are two spiritual lessons relative to this biblical encounter:

(a) The rich young man was not only imperfect with the things of God, but he also lacked the greatest thing/commandment; and as such, he lacked everything. In that story, the rich young man was not willing to forsake everything for the love of God. And since he was unwilling to forsake all the things of this world to follow Jesus, he could not truly say he loved God with all his heart, soul, and strength above everything else, for he preferred the gift to the Giver. As it is written, "If anyone desires to come after Me, let him deny himself, and take up his cross daily, and follow Me. For whoever desires to save his life will lose it, but whoever loses his life for My sake will save it. For what profit is it to a man if he gains the whole world, and is himself, destroyed or lost?" (Lk 9:23-25); (b) Again, the rich young man lacked the second great commandment—the love for others as God loved him. Since he was not freely willing to part with his worldly possessions for the love for others, he demonstrated that he did not love others as himself or as God loved him; hence, he considered his worldly possession more important and valuable than the love for God and others. This is so since giving to the poor is giving to God, the rich young man lacked the true love for God. For that, he (rich young man) woefully failed the test of love of God.

Of course, we must not rush into judgment against the rich young man, being mindful of the enormous dilemma he was confronted with. But the story demonstrated to us how fragile most of us are when we are confronted with a serious test or trial of our love of God. That is why the Lord left us, with no doubt, of the all-important nature of this spiritual hunger for God. "If anyone comes to Me and does not hate his father and mother, wife and children, brothers and sisters, yes, and his own life also, he cannot be My disciple" (Lk 14:26). To clarify this point the more, the Lord again said, "So likewise, whoever of you does not forsake all that he has he cannot be My disciple" (Lk 14:33). The two scripture verses just cited above are very widely misunderstood, exaggerated, and misused as manipulative instrument or tool in the hands of unscrupulous people. We know the Lord never asked us to hate or cut off all our relations or to forsake all things. Rather, He was driving this one important point home—that is, we do not love God with everything in and about us and, therefore, not worthy for the kingdom of God if there is possibly any person or thing or circumstance that takes precedence over God in our lives. If there is anything that we are not truly and readily willing to give up for the sake of the love we have for God, then we do not truly love Him. It is an all-or-nothing relationship, for our God is a jealous God who does not share His glory with any man or thing. The early apostles of the Lord truly demonstrated this spiritual hunger for God, and by so doing, they left us with examples to follow. In the Gospel of Matthew 4, we read that when Jesus asked Peter and his brother, Andrew, to follow Him, they left everything and followed Him (see Mt 4:18-20). And that was the same with the apostle John and his brother, James. They left all, including their father, and followed Him. "And immediately they left the boat and their father, and followed Him" (Mt 4:22). The apostle Matthew did the same when the Lord asked him to follow Him.

SEEKING GOD WITH ALL OUR HEARTS

From the beginning, God had revealed to us the nature of the spiritual hunger for Him that yields the right result: "And you will seek Me and find Me, when you search for Me with all your heart." (Jer 29:13). So merciful is our God that He never leaves us without examples to follow. By way of demonstration, He used His friend Abraham when He asked him to offer his only son (heir) as a sacrifice to Him. Because Abraham was willing to sacrifice his only son out of burning spiritual hunger for God and never valued what God gave him as above God, God blessed him above all humans. And He said, "Do not lay your hand on the lad, or do anything to him; for now I know that you fear God, since you have not withheld your son, your only son, from Me" (Gn 22:12). Abraham demonstrated his absolute love of and hunger for God; and God commands us to do the same.

Again, as a demonstration of His absolute love for us, God sacrificed everything for those who mean everything to Him. "For God so loved the world that He gave His only begotten Son, that whoever believes in Him should not perish but have everlasting life" (Jn 3:16). The question then is, what is God worth to you? If God is worth everything to you, you ought to give everything to seek Him and His righteousness. This is the only and most needful thing that is imperishable; for in truth, we shall inevitably leave and forsake all and be forsaken by all. The day will soon come when none of us will remember our businesses, jobs, wealth, children, and parents, etc. For it is written that we are appointed to die once and then to be subjected to judgment before the Lord of Lords. It is certainly true then that everyone must surely repent one way or the other. It is either repentance to life now or regret in hell later. The painful thing is that in most cases, we rebel, resist, and offend God with what He has graciously given us, thereby valuing the gift more than the Giver.

THE FIRST AND THE LAST

Let me share with you some mysteries surrounding the spiritual hunger for God. During one of the church-revival programs, the Lord told me to tell the congregation to be the first and the last. You can imagine the initial reaction of the congregation. There was murmuring and near-open disagreement. How could God ask them to be the first and the last? After all, the scripture warned, "But many who are first will be last, and the last first" (Mt 19:30). And that is not a blessing, but a curse. Nonetheless, God wanted to open the spiritual eyes of His children so they could understand the mysteries and the enduring nature of the race to His kingdom.

The truly born of God must be the first and the last in their relationship with God. They must seek God as early as with the most treasured, valued jewel (possession), and when they find Him, they must endure with Him even if they are the only ones left at the end. That which is most desired and valued must be sought after very early, and if you get it, you must hold on to it very jealously to the end. It is one thing finding a treasure and another thing keeping and preserving it to the end.

To show the mystery of this revelation, the Lord told me to ask the congregation what they knew and thought about Mary Magdalene. The response of that congregation and all other churches the Lord has sent me was unanimous. There were actually two things that the congregation remembered about Mary Magdalene: "adulterous sinner" and "the lady whom our Lord cast out seven devils from." But are those the only reasons why she is highly remembered and prominently memorized in the Bible? Was she the only sinner who had her devils cast out? The Lord told me that besides the mother of the Lord, no other woman was honored and blessed as Mary Magdalene. She was the first person the Lord appeared and spoke to following His resurrection from the dead. Mary Magdalene was neither an apostle nor one of the bigwigs of this world, yet in one particular incident, she was more than all because she was the first and the last in demonstration of spiritual hunger (love) for the Lord.

The scriptures tell us that while Christ was being buried, Mary Magdalene was at the sepulture, preparing the body for burial. At the approach of the Sabbath, she hurried home to wait for the end of the Sabbath. As soon as the Sabbath was over, even before the dawn of the day, this poor woman was the first to go to the tomb to see about the body of the Lord. "Now on the first day of the week Mary Magdalene went to the tomb early, while it was still dark" (Jn 20:1). I would bet that she never slept all night in anticipation of the end of the Sabbath. On getting to the tomb and finding it empty, she ran and reported her discovery to the apostles. Then, apostles Peter (the Rock) and John (the Beloved) ran with her to the tomb and found the tomb empty. These pillars of the church went back to their homes, but Mary Magdalene refused to give up. "Then the disciples went away again to their own homes. But Mary stood outside by the tomb weeping" (Jn 20:10-11). This poor woman refused to leave the tomb without the body of the Lord; and she wept bitterly for and demanded of it from everyone who entered her path. The Lord could not help but reveal Himself to Mary—a woman who loved and sought so much for Him, being the first and the last, and was not deterred or discouraged by the reactions of others. For that reason, Mary Magdalene is forever remembered as the first human who had the exclusive honor of seeing the Lord following His resurrection. Again, the Lord said to me, "The congregation should not murmur, for I am the first and the last, and all those born of Me ought to be the first and the last." Thus says the Lord, the King of Israel, and his redeemer, the Lord of Hosts, "I am the first and I am the Last; besides Me there is no God" (Is 44:6). "Listen to me, O Jacob, and Israel, My called: I am He, I am the First, I am also the Last" (Is 48:12). "I am the Alpha and the Omega, the Beginning and the End, the First and the Last" (Rv 22:13).

We must therefore seek God when we can find Him with all within and without us, and that time is now. We must be immovable to the end, even at the face of opposition, betrayal, and tribulations, or death. Let not the love of the truth ever forsake you and do not hesitate to forsake those things that are temporary and perishable, for the only needful and permanent treasure is in heaven. "Again, the kingdom of heaven is like treasure hidden in a field, which a man found and hid; and for joy over it he goes and sells all that he has and buys that field" (Mt 13:44).

RECIPROCITY

God reciprocates to every level of spiritual hunger we have for Him. In other words, like every other thing, we get what we put in our hunger/love for God. We certainly cannot honestly expect five pieces of potatoes at dinner when in reality we only boiled four pieces. God responds to us according to the intensity of our spiritual hunger for Him. When God sees that heart which is seeking Him above everything else and not willing to ever give up, He manifests Himself greatly to that heart. In the ordinary life, we intend to naturally gravitate to the people who truly love us, we trust them as friends, we cannot ordinarily pass by their neighborhood without stopping by to see them, and we freely confer with, and confide in them. This reciprocal relationship has been ever so with God from the beginning. In Genesis 18, we read that while God was on His way to destroy Sodom and Gomorrah, He had to detour to His friend's (Abraham) house. It was such a close friendship that made God confide in Abraham what He was about to do. And the Lord said, "Shall I hide from Abraham what I am doing?" (Gn 18:17). What an enviable relationship between God and man, and all because Abraham loved God above all things. Will you be another Abraham? As with Abraham and the encounter with the resurrected Christ by Mary Magdalene, another striking example is found in the story of Zacchaeus, in the Gospel of Luke 19. Zacchaeus was the short rich man who was so desirous/hungry to see Jesus that he had to run ahead and climb a tree. Reciprocating, the Lord's reaction was obvious. And when Jesus came to the place, He looked up and saw him and said to him, "Zacchaeus, make haste and come down, for today I must stay at your house" (Lk 19:5). It is interesting to note that although Jesus was just passing through Jericho, He could not ignore this one person who was so hungry for Him. He had to detour to Zacchaeus's house.

Another mystery of God's reciprocity to the spiritual hunger for Him is found in the Gospel of John 11. One day, while I was ministering in Africa, the Lord asked if I knew why Jesus wept for the first time. And my confident response was that Jesus wept because Lazarus, the one He loved, was dead. This is the same answer I get whenever I ask the same question to congregations. The Lord told me that was the wrong answer. How could Jesus weep for Lazarus's death when that death was designed by God to glorify both the Father and the Son? Besides, the Lord said that He would go to Bethany to raise Lazarus from the dead. There was therefore no cause for Him to weep for Lazarus; rather, He had every cause to rejoice. When Jesus heard of Lazarus's condition, he said, "This sickness is not unto death, but for the glory of God, that the Son of God might be glorified through it" (Jn 11:4). Again, He said to His disciples, "Our friend Lazarus sleeps, but I go that I may wake him up" (Jn 11:11). But when Mary (Lazarus's sister, the same Mary who sat at the feet of Jesus to hear the word and the same Mary who anointed the Lord with ointment and wiped His feet with her hair) fell at Jesus's feet weeping, Jesus, seeing the one who loved Him so much in agony, was moved and groaned in the spirit and wept. "Therefore, when Jesus saw her weeping. He groaned in the spirit and was troubled" (Jn 11:33) (see also Jn 11:32, 34-35). It is noteworthy that Martha (Mary's sister) had already seen and wept before the Lord, but her tears did not move the Lord to groan in the spirit (Jn 11:20-26).

It is the same when we share the agony of a beloved child or friend. But with a stranger, it may not be so. Also, the level of our spiritual hunger/love for God determines how much we are forgiven. "Therefore I say to you, her sins, which are many, are forgiven, for she loved much. But to whom little is forgiven, the same loves little." (Lk 7:47). Therefore, this is a new commandment: be the first and the last in your relationship with God.

Chapter Seven

LOVE FOR OTHERS

Whether we want to admit it or not, the most problematic area for over 99 percent of those who profess to be Christians is the love of others as ourselves, and it is even impossible to comprehend the concept of loving our enemies. For a born of God, the bar is raised a little higher with a new commandment to love others as God has loved us. That is, if it is possible, we should love others more than we love ourselves. This is the new commandment the Lord gave to us (see Jn 13:34). How did Jesus Christ love us? "Greater love has no one than this, than to lay down one's life for his friends" (Jn 15:13). It is when we are perfect in love that we can be said to be truly born of God and disciples of Jesus Christ. "By this all will know that you are My disciples, if you have love for one another" (Jn 13:35). While commanding us to love our enemies, the Lord said that it was what would differentiate us from the children of the devil if we are perfect (in love) as our heavenly Father is. "But I say to you, love your enemies, bless those who curse you, do good to those who hate you, and pray for those who spitefully use you and persecute you, that you may be sons of your Father in heaven; for He makes His sun rise on the evil and on the good, and sends rain on the just and on the unjust" (Mt 5:44-45). And why should we be as our heavenly Father? There certainly should be a remarkable difference between the children of God and those of the devil. The children of God walk in agreement with God with the necessary Godly attributes, and we cannot say we are one with Him when we are different in works contrary to Him. "For if you love those who love you, what reward have you? Do not even the tax collectors do the same? And if you greet your brethren only, what do you do more than others? Do not even the tax collectors do so?" (Mt 5:46-47).

Therefore, the only way we can walk with God as His children is to be in perfect agreement with Him. "Therefore you shall be perfect, just as your Father in heaven is perfect" (Mt 5:48).

Sadly, most of us, by our actions, walk contrary to the commandment and doctrine of our Lord Jesus Christ. Some either still practice "an eye for and eye" or pay lip service to love, having their hearts hardened and darkened while conditioning their love upon some worldly gain or reward and, amazingly, able to freely, without godly conscience, switch from one extreme of love to another extreme of hate in a moment of time; yet they appear to live in churches. Some love only their own kind, or members, while others hide their hatred with smiles. And still, in abominable fashion, most Christians, including ministers of the Gospel, especially in developing countries, preach and encourage "eye for an eye" for their own selfish gain, teaching and fiercely defending this anti-Christ doctrine.

In an attempt to correct the above-mentioned ills among Christians and to get God's children to return to the love of the truth of the true Gospel and doctrine of our Lord, Jesus Christ, this chapter may take a life of its own in substance and length. Because many of us bring daily curses upon ourselves by resorting to doing the works of the law, which our Lord died and rose to deliver us from such bondage. "Love your enemies"—easier said than done. Rather than seriously believing in this commandment and asking God for His Spirit to help us made perfect in love, we take the easier road by employing every excuse, tactic, and interpretation to rationalize our rebellious disobedience. I do not believe that among Christians, you can find, at most, 1 percent who truly believe and practice this commandment—just as there may not be up to 1 percent of Christians who are truly born of God and now ready (this instant) for the coming of the Lord. Some hold strongly that no human can love as God loves. While this position has an enormous weight to it, it is nevertheless biblically incorrect. Perhaps the better assertion is that no flesh is capable of being perfect in love as God is. Indeed, there is no human who is capable of truly loving his enemies, except one who is born of God and led by His Spirit. God, who knows all things, cannot lie, for He commands us to be holy and perfect as He is—knowing fully well that without His enabling and transforming Spirit, we can do nothing. All things are possible to those who believe. These are the children of God who are given to understand the mysteries of His kingdom. They are those transformed into His image, and created after God in righteousness and holiness. They are gods; and as gods they are commanded to be perfect in love as God is (See Mt 5:48). These people are the elect of God who have been given the power to become children of God and understand the mysteries of His kingdom. To those who are the called of God and true disciples of the Lord, He answered and said to them, "Because it has been given to you to know the mysteries of the kingdom of heaven, but to them it has not been given" (Mt 13:11).

Again, when the disciples of the Lord expressed their amazement at what He said relative to the rich, He said to them, "With men this is impossible, but with God all things are possible" (Mt 19:26). If we are sincerely willing to forsake our evil ways and obey God with a humble heart, He has promised to give us a new spirit to do that which is impossible for the flesh and blood to do. As already stated, he who is born of the flesh is flesh, and he who is born of the spirit is spirit (see Jn 3:6). And as is written, so he answered and said to me, "This is the word of the Lord to Zerubbabel: 'Not by might nor by power, but by My Spirit,' Says the Lord of hosts. 'Who are you, O Great Mountain? Before Zerubbabel you shall become plain! And he shall bring forth the capstone with shouts of "Grace, grace to it!"'" (Zec 4:6-7). For those who are given by God and led by His Spirit, they are under a new commandment to be as perfect in love as God. It is neither doing to others as they do to us nor loving our neighbors as we love ourselves (see Mt 7:12; Lev 19:18). Rather, by loving others as God loves us, people will readily know that we are true disciples of Jesus Christ, for Christ loved us more than He loved Himself; and for that, He gave Himself for us. A careful study of apostle Paul's First Epistle to the Corinthians in chapter 13 (1 Cor 13) gives a vivid picture of the kind of love for others, which is expected of those who are true children of God—the kind of love that is perfect unto God. "Love suffers long and is kind; love does not envy; love does not parade itself, is not puffed up; does not behave rudely, does not seek its own, is not provoked, thinks no evil; does not rejoice in iniquity, but rejoices in the truth; bears all things, endures all things" (1 Cor 13:4-7).

Unlike spiritual gifts, perfect love is a fruit of the Spirit that never fails (see 1 Cor 13:8). We should desire, at all cost, the imperishable fruits of the Spirit more than the gifts that pass away with time. Besides the Lord, examples of perfect love abound in the Holy Bible of which include, but not limited to, Abraham's love for Lot, Joseph's love for his brothers, Moses's love for Israel, and Ruth's love for Naomi. However, one striking demonstration of perfect love was exhibited by Jonathan, the son of King Saul. It was obvious that Jonathan loved David more than he loved himself. In that, he loved David even to his own detriment, knowing as it were that as long as David lived, he (Jonathan, the rightful heir to the throne) would not succeed his father. Yet he swore perfect love to David with his life (see 1 Sm 20:12-42). As it is written, so Jonathan made a covenant with the house of David, saying, "Let the Lord require it at the hands of David's enemies" (1 Sm 20:16). Jonathan loved David as he loved his own soul (see 1 Sm 20:17). We are of Christ if we obey all He has commanded us. And what did our Lord command us to do? Love our enemies and avenge not ourselves. One who is not perfect in love has not a pure heart and is not born of God, for God is love (see 1 Jn 4:16, 18). It is also written that anyone who claims to be of God and hates another is yet in darkness: "He who says he is in the light, and hates his brother, is in darkness until now. He who loves his brother abides in the light, and there is no cause for stumbling in him" (1 Jn 2:9-10).

AVENGE NOT

Oh! How much easier said than done? This is one of the most difficult things to get humans to accept, let alone get them to do. Hence, even most of us employ every excuse, trick, and justification in the book to obtain "sweet revenge." Vengeance, including dangerous and evil prayers against enemies (real or perceived), is the satisfaction of the devilish craving of the proud, wicked, and uncircumcised heart of man. For those who are born of God, they must not only leave vengeance to God, but they are also under spiritual obligation to plead to God to forgive and save the evildoer. They are able to do this because they are led by the Spirit of God, which dwells in them; having acquired a new heart, mind, body, and spirit and therefore able to obey all the commandments of God, one of which clearly says, "You shall not take vengeance, nor bear any grudge against the children of your people, but you shall love your neighbor as yourself: I am the Lord" (Lv 19:18). "Vengeance is Mine, and recompense . . ." (Dt 32:35).

Whoever takes vengeance (retaliates) has taken matters into his own hands, and whoever takes matters into his own hands is not born of God. For even though we live, not us but Christ lives in us; and if Christ lives in us, then we are Christ's and therefore ought to do the works of Christ and walk as He walked (see Jn 14:12; 1 Jn 2:6). While the Lord was on earth, He taught and lived the exact words and commandments of the Father who sent Him. When He suffered, He avenged not; was forsaken, He loved; was reviled, He reviled not; was cursed, He blessed; was crucified, He forgave. Yet today and forever, He is the King of Kings and Lord of Lords. To claim or profess to be of Christ and yet act contrary to His commandments is heresy. But most Christians, especially in developing nations, would rather preach, encourage, cite, and practice the works of the Old Testament scripture of "an eye for an eye," "suffer not the witch to live," and the judgment and condemnation of every tongue raised against them. Yet they cannot claim that they have not heard the Lord who came down from heaven to show the way. "You have heard that it was said, 'An eye for an eye and a tooth for a tooth.' But I tell you not to resist an evil person. But whoever slaps you on your right cheek, turn the other to him also" (Mt 5:38-39).

Again, "You have heard that it was said, 'You shall love your neighbor and hate your enemy.' But I say to you, love your enemies, bless those who curse you, do good to those who hate you, and pray for those who spitefully use you and persecute you" (Mt 5:43-44). These Christians who practice and teach the old works of the law forget that the scriptures are in harmony and devoid of contradictions. It is not possible for the omnipotent and all-knowing God to contradict Himself. It is not possible for God to command us both to avenge and not avenge. For evil, no matter how we dress and justify it, is an abomination to God. The New Testament scriptures are filled with loving and returning good for evil. Jesus Christ is the only way to the Father, and He was sent by the Father to show us that only way to righteousness and holiness. The apostle Paul, in adherence to the strict doctrine of Jesus Christ, admonished, thus: "Bless those who persecute you; bless and do not curse" (Rom 12:14). "Beloved, do not avenge yourselves, but rather give place to wrath; for it is written, 'Vengeance is Mine, I will repay,' says the Lord" (Rom 12:19). And again, "Do not be overcome by evil, but overcome evil with good" (Rom 12:21).

The above are the prescribed ways of God for His children. God and the devil have nothing in common. God has His own method for victorious Christian living. The greatest weapon in God's arsenal is perfect love, which overcomes all evils.

Therefore, praying to God against one's enemies as most Christians do is dangerous and evil. Those who take vengeance or engage in dangerous evil prayers and curses against their enemies are yet doing the works of the law and under a curse; and as such, the coming, death, and resurrection of our Lord are in vain for them. "For as many as are of the works of the law are under the curse; for it is written, 'Cursed is everyone who does not continue in all things which are written in the book of the law, to do them'" (Gal 3:10). And why are they under curse? Because "Christ has redeemed us from the curse of the law, having become a curse for us [for it is written, "Cursed is everyone who hangs on a tree"]" (Gal 3:13). As it is also written, "For Christ is the end of the law for righteousness to every one who believes" (Rom 10:4). For if we avenge, we do evil; and there is no good or justified evil. Evil plus evil is double evil, which brings death. It is a simple equation: $e + e = 2e = d$. "As righteousness leads to life, so he who pursues evil pursues it to his own death" (Prv 11:19).

Again, it is written, "Tribulation and anguish, on every soul of man who does evil, of the Jew first and also of the Greek" (Rom 2:9). It is the duty of God's children to fear Him, and the one significant way of demonstrating this fear is to abhor evil. "The fear of the Lord is to hate evil; pride and arrogance and the evil way and the perverse mouth, I hate" (Prv 8:13). Hatred for any kind of evil is bluntly amplified in the Bible, thus: "God is a just judge, and God is angry with the wicked every day" (Ps 7:11). But sadly, an infamous devilish belief is proudly quoted and practiced in some developing nations: "You do me bad and I do you bad, God no go vex" (if you do me evil and I avenge with evil, God will not be offended).

A common and popular evil prayer in just about every church in these places is calling on the Holy Ghost to send His fire against their enemies. This is commonly referred to as "Holy

Ghost Fire". What an abominable heresy and incompatible phenomenon of invoking the Holy Spirit of God to go and do evil. While the fire of the Spirit of God is a blessing, the devil has greatly gone into many churches to turn that which is holy into a means to blaspheme the Spirit of God. When questioned about his authority to baptize, John the Baptist said, among other things, that one greater than him would come, and He would baptize people with the Holy Ghost and with fire (see Mt 3:11).

Sadly, throughout my stay in Africa and in all the church-revival programs, the issue of loving your enemies and leaving vengeance to God provoked thunderous questions and arguments from both ministers and congregations. Some could not comprehend how they would let the one who is doing everything to destroy them, or who had already hurt them or their families walk free and unchallenged. But can the wicked ever be free? As we have already read, God is angry at the wicked every single day. But if we react to an evil deed with evil, we become evildoers since we are what we do. Evil can never be good; as the saying goes, "Two wrongs cannot make a right." There is no spiritual difference between an original evil act and a secondary retaliatory evil act. Instead of resolving the matter, two wrongs will complicate and compound it, ushering in a cyclical saga of curse and consuming death. While being pursued by the men of Joab, Abner, the commander of King Saul's army, called to Joab and said, "Shall the sword devour forever? Do you not know that it will be bitter in the latter end? How long will it be then until you tell the people to return from pursuing their brethren?" (2 Sm 2:26). On the same issue, the apostle Paul admonished the church of God at Galatia, thus: "But if you bite and devour one another, beware lest you be consumed by one another" (Gal 5:15). Besides, it is a wrong strategy to fight the enemy with his own weapon. The greatest weapon of the devil and his agents is evil. Therefore, a true child of God who engages or rewards evil for evil is a candidate marked for woeful defeat. You cannot fight the master with his own weapon. Rather, to defeat the enemy, you will have to employ a greater weapon than he has—*love*. Love is the language and weapon the devil cannot understand.

King David clearly understood this important commandment of God, so much so that even when God delivered his enemy (Saul) into his hands, he (David) refused to take vengeance, leaving the righteous God to judge between him and King Saul. And why does God command us to leave vengeance to Him? God does not want anyone's blood on His children's hands. He is God; He can do what pleases Him. But for us, we cannot remain guiltless for any evil deed we do. Again, David got it perfectly right when he answered his followers who were urging him to kill King Saul. But David said to Abishai, "Do not destroy him; for who can stretch out his hand against the Lord's anointed, and be guiltless?" (1 Sm 26:9). As we have already read in the book of Proverbs, whoever pursues evil pursues it to his death (see Prv 11:19). The truth of this scripture was exemplified in the book of Ezekiel 25, where God pronounced harsher judgment against Edom and the Philistines for taking vengeance against Israel. Thus says the Lord God, "Because the Philistines dealt vengefully and took vengeance with a spiteful heart, to destroy because of the old hatred. I will stretch out My hand against the Philistines, and I will cut off the Cherethites and destroy the remnant of the seacoast. I will execute great vengeance on them with furious rebukes; and they shall know that I am the Lord, when I lay My vengeance upon them" (Ez 25:15-17).

Very consistently again God cursed Cain and sent him out of the face of the earth, yet he forbade anyone from avenging the death of Abel. "Therefore, whoever kills Cain, vengeance shall be taken on him sevenfold" (Gn 4:15). There is therefore a harsher punishment against the avenger than the initial evildoer. This is so, because vengeance/retaliation is usually executed with a spiteful and premeditated evil heart, desired to inflict severer hurt. Hence, the scriptures seriously warned us to flee from taking vengeance.

The question many still ask to this day is: What then was the purpose of the harsh Old Testament provisions against wicked and evil people? The apostle Paul pointedly addressed this concern for us. As is written: "What purpose then does the law serve? It was added because of transgressions, till the seed should come to whom the promise was made; and it was appointed through angels by the hand of a mediator" (Gal 3: 19). Expatiating further, the apostle Paul writes: "But before faith came, we were kept under guard by the law, kept for the faith which would afterward be revealed. Therefore the law was our tutor to bring us to Christ, that we might be justified by faith. But after faith has come, we are no longer under a tutor" (Gal 3: 23-25). Jesus Christ is the fulfillment of the law and the beginning of the new covenant relationship, which God had promised. To ensure consistency with His commandments, our Lord took the time to state clearly to us: "You have heard that it was said, 'an eye for an eye and a tooth for a tooth'" "But I tell you not to resist an evil person . . ." (Mt 5: 38-39). Therefore, as is written: "But if you are led by the Spirit, you are not under the law" (Gal 5: 18). And as we have already read, those who are led by God's Spirit are His true children; and whoever is not led by His Spirit is none of His (see Rom 8: 9, 14). God's Spirit is a Spirit of perfect love and implicit obedience.

If any reader is still not clear on this very important issue, then let him or her answer these two questions: who is Jesus Christ, and who are we? If we truly believe that Jesus Christ is the only begotten Son of God who came from heaven to show the way and we are His true disciples (Christians), then it is a no-brainer that we ought to walk as He walked, by way of obedience to His commandments. If we are true followers and friends of Christ, we should obey and adhere strictly to all He has commanded us (see Jn 15:14). It means that those who go contrary to His commandments and doctrine are against Him. As the Lord said, "My sheep hear My voice, and I know them, and they follow Me" (Jn 10:27). Therefore, the children of God hear only God's voice and do not succumb to confusing voices of the devil and his agents (see Jn 8:47). They live every word of God (see Dt 8:3). He who has ear in his heart to hear let him hear.

THE OTHER GREAT EVIL

Now there is another greater evil than praying and wishing your enemies' evil. This is common among Christians in the developed world. These are people who nicely hide their hatred with a smile. These are the more dangerous elements, whose hearts and their mouths are in conflict. Inside, they are bottled up with hatred and evil while outwardly manifesting their fake love. These receive greater damnation, for they are hypocrites; for out of the abundance of their hearts, their mouths speak falsehood, deceit, lies, and flattery. As is written, "Woe to you, scribes and Pharisees, hypocrites! For you cleanse the outside of the cup and dish, but inside they are full of extortion and self-indulgence" (Mt 23:25). "Woe to you, scribes and Pharisees, hypocrites! For you are like whitewashed tombs which indeed appear beautiful outwardly, but inside are full of dead men's bones and all uncleanness" (Mt 23:27). "Even so you also outwardly appear righteous to men, but inside you are full of hypocrisy and lawlessness" (Mt 23:28). Therefore says the scripture, "He that hideth hatred with lying lips, and he that uttereth a slander, is a fool" (AV, Prv 10:18).

All these are not written to judge or condemn anyone but that the children of God may examine their hearts with a view to mending their ways before it is too late. For no one with an evil heart can see God. Hence, the scripture clearly says, "Blessed are the pure in heart, for they shall see God" (Mt 5:8).

SPIRITUAL ATTITUDE

Now if we are born of God and led by His Spirit (spirit of love, compassion, forgiveness, reconciliation, and obedience), which is the new spirit in Christ, we should have spiritual eye and attitude toward afflictions and evil deeds; for the Spirit of God, which dwells in us, enables us to understand that evildoers lack knowledge (knowledge of God) and, therefore, are lost and sick. As such, we are under obligation, as disciples of the Light, to ask God from our heart to forgive the one who lacks knowledge and to show the lost the way, mostly by what we do and how we react to their evil deeds. Even when God's vengeance is inevitable (for every act receives recompense), we should intercede for them, being always consciously mindful that not too long ago we were like them. It is incumbent on us, therefore, to extend love, grace, and mercy to all. You can correctly assert that no human being is capable of doing this, and you are right. There is no human capable of being perfect in love, except the one who is born of and led by the Spirit of God; and we know that with God, all things are possible. Again, no one can understand the mysteries of God until it is given to him or her.

Chapter Eight

THE TESTS OF LOVE OF OTHERS

Love, like any other thing, cannot be certified as true, perfect, and godly until it is tested and proven, just as you will not graduate and be certified until you pass the requisite tests. In this chapter, we will examine just a few of the critical tests of love for others.

LOVE WITH ACTION

Similar to the Epistle of James 2:15-17, "If a brother or sister is naked and destitute of daily food, and one of you says to them, 'Depart in peace, be warmed and filled,' but you do not give them the things which are needed for the body, what does it profit? Thus also faith by itself, if it does not have works, is dead." So love without action is dead on arrival. Many of us are good at using empty vocabularies of love, but when the actual test comes, we are found wanting. If you think you have more friends and relations than you can handle, wait until you find yourself in an unenviable position, and you will find soon enough if you actually even have a single friend or relation indeed. Writing from experience, I confess that, truly, there is no friend like Jesus. And if by God's grace you have one faithful and loyal friend indeed who dares to draw near you when you are in the wilderness, blessed are you and your friend. Such friend or relation is a rare gift from God.

Those born of God ought to give even the very shirt off their backs to a brother or anyone in need. Otherwise, our expression of love will be like a sweet, feel-good doctrine that has no true spiritual substance/value. It is like a cloud without rain or a hollow tree that falls at the slightest touch of the wind. As the apostle John wrote in his First Epistle, "But whoever has this world's goods, and sees his brother in need, and shuts up his heart from him, how does the love of God abide in him? My little children let us not love in word or in tongue, but in deed and in truth" (3:17-18). Similarly, while we may profess all our love for God, it is meaningless without action and obedience. The only way to prove we love Him is to obey all He has commanded us. As is written, "If you love Me, keep My commandments" (Jn 14:15). "But that the world may know that I love the Father, and as the Father gave Me commandment, so I do. Arise, let us go from here" (Jn 14:31). The Lord himself highlighted this real love and compassion in the parable of the Good Samaritan (see Lk 10:30-37).

As we read, neither an ordained priest nor a Levite showed love but a Samaritan, who showed mercy and compassion to the one in need; and for that, he was justified. As for the later individuals, although they believed they were nearer to God than others, they nevertheless woefully failed the crucial test of love. "For with their mouth they show much love, but their hearts pursue their own gain" (Ez 33:31).

The easy excuse for some of us is that we have nothing to give. But we forget—or rather, do not understand—that we all have more than enough to give others. What is the greatest gift we can give to others? To answer this question, we must first answer, what is man's greatest need? The greatest need, I believe, is eternal life (salvation). So even if you do not have any physical thing to give, you can give the gift of life, for we are called to bear fruit (see Jn 15:16). And he who wins souls is not only wise but blessed. Therefore, the children of God have more than enough to offer. They can offer that which is not perishable (salvation and prayers). And they have that which unbelievers can never have—the authority and power of Jesus Christ that breaks every yoke.

In the Acts of the Apostles, although the apostles Peter and John had no tangible physical things to give to the lame man at the gate of the temple, they gave the man what he needed, which was more than he wanted. Then, Peter said, "Silver and gold I do not have, but what I do have I give you: In the name of Jesus Christ of Nazareth, rise up and walk" (3:6). The lame man got a new lease on life. Therefore, the greatest gift is love, and God is love.

Incidentally, the characteristic of the greatest gift is that it is free, but priceless. "Ho! Everyone who thirsts, Come to the waters; And you who have no money, Come, buy and eat. Yes, come, buy wine and milk Without money and without price. Why do you spend money for what is not bread, and your wages for what does not satisfy?" (Is 55:1-2). The preceding scripture is consistent with our Lord's gracious invitation for us to accept His easy yoke and light burden (see Mt 11:28-30). Therefore, if nothing else, the children of God should give the gift of perfect love.

LAUGHING AT ANOTHER'S CALAMITY

This is a very troublesome test of love for others, especially our *enemies*. Most of us profess and boast of our maturity in loving and forgiving others until some calamity strikes our enemies, then the bottom falls, and we woefully fail this spiritual test. Some of us laugh very loudly and say, "Aha, he has got what he deserves." And we even enjoy amplifying the fall of our enemies and others. One who is born of God mourns for those in difficulties, no matter the circumstances. He communes with God in intercession for them. Even those on death row, convicted of the most heinous crimes, and those mortal enemies who appear to be born for our hurt and torment, they all deserve our love, compassion, and prayers; for as a spiritual truth, they do not know what they do.

Whoever is not led by the Spirit of God lacks knowledge of God and is therefore lost and dead. Those who are the light of God on the earth ought to mourn for them, not laugh at them. It grieves God to see His child suffer calamities, but it grieves Him more to see another laughing at His child. "Do I have any pleasure at all that the wicked should die?" says the Lord God. "And not that he should turn from his ways and live?" (Ez 18:23).

Just as with any earthly parent who may say to a rebellious child in trouble, "I told you so!" but in reality he or she is grieving for the suffering child. Then imagine if a stranger comes along to mock and laugh at that child. I bet the parent would not take it kindly. God does not rejoice but rather grieves when His child is in trouble, no matter the circumstances that brought about the trouble. It was this fatherly love and compassion that led God to send His only begotten Son to die for us.

The Tests of Love of Others

Therefore, whoever laughs at another's calamity hates, laughs at, and mocks God; and such mockery will not go unpunished. "He who mocks the poor reproaches his Maker; He who is glad at calamity will not go unpunished." (Prv 17:5). Worse still, God may turn away the calamity of the sufferer to the mocker. "Do not rejoice when your enemy falls, And do not let your heart be glad when he stumbles; Lest the Lord see it, and it displease Him, And He turn away His wrath from him" (Prv 24:17-18).

The Lord demonstrated His wrath against the Ammonites and Moabites for laughing at the calamity of Israel. "Say to the Ammonites, 'Hear the word of the Lord God! Thus says the Lord God: "Because you said, 'Aha!' against My sanctuary when it was profaned, and against the land of Israel when it was desolate, and against the house of Judah when they went into captivity, indeed, therefore, I will deliver you as a possession to the men of the East, and they shall set their encampments among you and make their dwellings among you; they shall eat your fruit, and they shall drink your milk"' (Ez 25:3-4). For thus says the Lord God, "Because you clapped your hands, stamped your feet, and rejoiced in heart with all your disdain for the land of Israel, indeed, therefore, I will stretch out My hand against you, and give you as plunder to the nations; I will cut you off from the peoples, and I will cause you to perish from the countries; I will destroy you, and you shall know that I am the Lord" (Ez 25:6-7).

Those who have put on Christ, as new creatures, ought to love others as He loved them. "For to this you were called, because Christ also suffered for us, leaving us an example, that you should follow His steps" (1 Pt 2:21). "Who Himself bore our sins in His own body on the tree, that we, having died to sins, might live for righteousness—by whose stripes you were healed" (1 Pt 2:24). Therefore, a true born of God should bear others' burdens and share in their good and bad times. "Rejoice with those who rejoice, and weep with those who weep" (Rom 12:15). And the Bible says more, "Bear one another's burdens, and so fulfill the law of Christ" (Gal 6:2).

It is a true statement that laughing at another's calamities is an expression of hatred in our hearts toward the individual. Some of us claim that we are not laughing at someone when he falls, but we will not stop to amplify and broadcast another's trouble. If that is not mocking or laughing or downright unsympathetic, I do not know what it is. Whatever is done or said not out of love is not of God. The all-important question is, how does what I do or say help the sufferer and glorify God? How soon we forget that not too long ago, we were saved by grace and the Lord has graciously been covering our sins. Now, if God would let the lid off, some of us would go to a different planet to escape our heinous past. If we are God's children, we should do God's works and be perfect and holy as He is. Therefore, have mercy on those who have stumbled and fallen so that you may obtain more mercy for the evil days, which tarry not.

ANGRY SITUATION

Another great test or measure of our love for others and spiritual maturity is in a given angry situation. Angry and annoying situations must surely come our way, no question about that. "These things I have spoken to you, that in Me you may have peace. In the world you will have tribulation; but be of good cheer, I have overcome the world" (Jn 16:33).

Who is he that has overcome the world, but he who is born of God? And how does he overcome the world, but with love? For God is love. Angry situations provide the ideal opportunity to measure our spiritual maturity, as well as test our true identity as born-again Christians. You can easily tell if one is under the restraint of the Holy Spirit in an angry situation. How we react to angry situations says a lot of who we are. Most of us appear as the sweetest human beings until our little toes are stepped upon, and we unleash brimstone from hell against the offender, thereby throwing all caution, love, compassion, and grace to the wind. If the Holy Spirit dwells in us, He will get us to sympathize with and have mercy on the wrongdoer because he lacks the spiritual knowledge of God. For if the offender knows God, he wouldn't do what he did. You are the light of the world, and at that time your light is being tested. If you react as the offender, you become as he is. How we react to angry situations differentiates us from the children of the devil. If therefore we act and react as unbelievers, we become as they are. "Do not answer a fool according to his folly, lest you also be like him" (Prv 26:4). Therefore, if in angry situations we speak and act or react like unbelievers, we are unbelievers. It is what we do that bears witness of us. "Even so, every good tree bears good fruit, but a bad tree bears bad fruit. Therefore by their fruits you will know them" (Mt 7:17, 20).

While I was in Africa, the Lord told me to ask the congregations to buy for themselves three critical things that would help them overcome angry situations:

1. A sewing machine to sew the tongue
2. A zipper to zip up the mouths
3. A chain leash for the waist

For a true born of God, if in the past you spoke ten words in a minute, especially in angry situations, now you should learn to speak only one word. Even at that, this one word must be the truth, and you should be careful how you say it to others; otherwise, it becomes sinful. An example will set this point straight. If I discover the wrong of a brother in a church and report it to the pastor just for the sole purpose of helping and restoring him to order, it is commendable. However, if I speak to everyone about the matter, I am no longer doing it out of love and not helping him, and that is sinful.

In an angry situation, the one who takes the matter into his own hands is not of God. We all agree that being angry is not sinful; after all, God gets angry. However, we are commanded not to let our anger be sinful. That is to say, let not your anger lead you to sin. "Be angry, and do not sin": do not let the sun go down on your wrath, nor give place to the devil" (Eph 4:26-27). There are four things that we can do that would make our anger sinful and grieve to the Holy Spirit:

    a. *Anger retention.* If we retain anger inside us for a longer time than necessary, it takes a few minutes for our heart to get so hardened in bitterness or pride that the Holy Spirit is grieved and departs, giving the devil easy access.

    b. *The tongue moves, and the mouth opens.* This evil duo, in angry situations, presents a constant challenge in our spiritual walk. As such, a duo protection of a sewing machine and a zipper is a necessity. If your tongue moves and your mouth opens in anger, you have given room to the devil. When two people are angry and arguing, each one is trying vigorously to prove that he or she is right,

The Tests of Love of Others

and the other person is wrong; and whatever one says in response to an angry situation is always intended to score the severer hurt. Every angry word we utter against another grieves the Holy Spirit, for we are the children of God, and all our words are to minister life, not death. If every idle word we speak subjects us to judgment, how much more of angry words? "But I say to you that for every idle word men may speak, they will give account of it in the day of judgment. For by your words you will be justified, and by your words you will be condemned" (Mt 12:36-37). This gives us the more reason why it is imperative for a true born of God to sew his tongue with a sewing machine and zip his mouth shut. For as the scripture says, "Whoever guards his mouth and tongue keeps his soul from troubles" (Prv 21:23). Because as the scripture further says, "Death and life are in the power of the tongue, and those who love it will eat its fruit" (Prv 18:21). Since the foul tongue defiles the entire body (for out of the heart the mouth speaks), the tongue, as part of the flesh, must be brought completely into subjection to the spirit, in the life of a born of God. "And the tongue is a fire, a world of iniquity. The tongue is so set among our members that it defiles the whole body, and sets on fire the course of nature; and it is set on fire by hell" (Jas 3:6). Again, the scripture tells us that the man who is quick to anger is a fool, but the one who is hasty to utter a word in anger is worse than a fool. "Do not hasten in your spirit to be angry, for anger rests in the bosom of fools" (Eccl 7:9). "Do you see a man hasty in his words? There is more hope for a fool than for him" (Prv 29:20).

c. *The hands and feet move.* If you kick with either hands or legs in angry situations, you give room to the devil. To avoid this, we need a chain leash of the Holy Spirit around our waist to always restrain us in angry situations. Therefore, always put on a leash against a trying day. And for some of us who are easily provoked into using our hands and legs as weapons in response to angry situations, a very short chain leash tied to a steel beam is highly recommended so that when we rant and rave like mad dogs, we nevertheless can't bite or scratch. Those who are born of God are of God and therefore gods. We know that God gets angry, but He reacts and handles anger with love. So the greatest thing we should always possess in whatsoever we do is love. Let everything a child of God does be done unto God and anchored on love, for God is love; and whatever is done not out of love is not of God. As gods, we are the light of the world and endued with spiritual attitude toward any tribulation or affliction. With a Godlike attitude, we accept every difficult situation or challenge as a blessing, an opportunity to glorify God's name and put the devil to shame. If we can subdue anger with love and rather exercise and extend mercy, grace, and compassion, we disarm the devil and put him to shame. By so doing, we also heap tormenting guilt on the offender's conscience (not hot coals to burn his head as some love to interpret that provision of the scripture). For if we heap hot burning coal on the heads of those who offend us, we manifest vengeance and evil, which is ungodly and wicked.

Chapter Nine

WHERE TWO OR THREE ARE GATHERED IN HIS NAME

At one of the church-revival programs/conferences in Africa, I asked the Lord what He would want me to tell the church on the first day of the program, and the Lord said to me, "Tell them that where two or three are gathered in My name, I am not there." What a shocker. You can imagine my reaction. I was disturbed and wondered seriously if that was the Lord speaking to me. Then the Lord said again to me, "When you get to the church, stand before the congregation and tell them that where two or three are gathered in My name, I am not there, and you will find that although they profess to gather in My name, but not all together in My name. For how could they gather together in My name when they are not in agreement and with one mind? I am the Prince of Peace, and where there is no peace, I am not there. When you get there, you will find out they have gathered in My name, but not by Me." Sure enough, when I delivered the message of the Lord, the pastors and leaders of the church were in tears while admitting that the Lord touched on the biggest problem threatening the very existence of the church and the entire denomination, which it belonged to.

At the conclusion of the service, there was the traditional call for members to wish one another well. And as that tradition was going on, I could see clearly a pattern of ungodly behavior among the members of the same church. Some members smiled and happily embraced their friends or those of them belonging to their clique while they frowned and made faces at others who were not their favorites. A house divided indeed.

While things may not be exactly similar with other churches and denominations as the church discussed, it is an indisputable fact that most houses of God have become houses of merchandise, envy, discord, rancor, personal pursuit, conflict, manipulation, deceit, and lies. So divided it beats every imagination. As such, some churches and denominations are operated in the model of security outfits where members are monitored, and all means are employed to control and bring members to check. They profess to gather in the name of the Lord, but not together in agreement with Him. It is obvious that the most segregated day of the week is Sunday, when everyone goes to his or her own little church while love is left outside. When we do not gather (in agreement) in Christ, our gathering in His name is in vain; at worst, hypocritical, and at best, blasphemous. Division, strife, envy, greed, etc., are signs of carnality, which is enmity toward God. "For you are still carnal. For where there are envy, strife, and divisions among you, are you not carnal and behaving like mere men?" (1 Cor 3:3).

The greatest desire and prayer of our Lord before and after His death was for His disciples to be one—in the unity of one mind and one purpose. There is only one Christ and one God, the Father, and one doctrine. Therefore, disunity, division, envy, and strife are not testimonies that we are of Christ and that He was sent by the Father to show the way, and that He came so that He might make perfect in one with Him and with each other. "Now I am no longer in the world, but these are in the world, and I come to You. Holy Father, keep through Your name those whom You have given Me, that they may be one as We are. I in them, and You in Me, that they may be made perfect in one, and that the world may know that You have sent Me, and have loved them as You have loved Me" (Jn 17:11, 23).

When there is disagreement, division, strife, and even hatred among the churches of God, how can we say that we are of Christ, for the world may not know that we are Christ sent? The apostle Paul strongly admonished the church of God, which was at Corinth, thus: "Now I plead with you, brethren, by the name of our Lord Jesus Christ, that you all speak the same thing, and that there be no divisions among you, but that you be perfectly joined together in the same mind and in the same judgment" (1 Cor 1:10).

The worst case is division and strife among ordained ministers who are fiercely deadlocked in ungodly competitions and witch-hunting against one another. While some of them may appear as one, they are nevertheless more divided as ever. Some harbor bitter hatred and ill will toward others. They have no restraint defaming other churches and denominations and even forbidding their members from any close contact with people of "different faith," as they refer to other denominations. They forbid interdenominational marriages because one of the partners is not a member of their flock and is therefore an unbeliever. But are Christians not supposed to be of one faith in Christ, one doctrine of Jesus Christ, one God the Father, and one Holy Spirit? As it is written, "There is one body and one Spirit, just as you were called in one hope of your calling; one Lord, one faith, one baptism; one God and Father of all, who is above all, and through all, and in you all" (Eph 4:4-6).

If we are working for the same master, for the same result, and under one doctrine, why do we have divisions, denominations, and strife among us? Some denominations and churches go to the wicked extent of excommunicating, with viciousness, any member who leaves to attend another denomination or church. It is quite obvious that denominational doctrine is of the devil, being man-fashioned for his personal gain and ambition. "Now I urge you, brethren, note those who cause divisions and offenses, contrary to the doctrine which you learned, and avoid them. For those who are such do not serve our Lord Jesus Christ, but their own belly, and by smooth words and flattering speech deceive the hearts of the simple" (Rom 16:17-18).

Unfortunately, some ministers of today's churches proceed to carve out their empires and run their own doctrine, devising every means to get members to feel good while discarding the love of the truth; they perfect Psychology 101, telling their captive audience what they (members) want to hear (not what God wants them to hear) so that, in return, they (ministers) will get what they want, thereby shoving aside the truth of the Gospel of Jesus Christ or, at best, compromising and watering down the Gospel of the kingdom of God. Every messenger of God, including our Lord Jesus Christ, warned us to beware of the proliferation of false ministers and prophets. "But there were also false prophets among the people, even as there will be false teachers among you, who will secretly bring in destructive heresies, even denying the Lord who bought them, and bring on themselves swift destruction. And many will follow their destructive ways, because of whom the way of truth will be blasphemed. By covetousness they will exploit you with deceptive words; for a long time their judgment has not been idle, and their destruction does not slumber" (2 Pt 2:1-3).

I am mindful of the fact I run the obvious risk of being misunderstood or labeled as a church or minister basher. It is not my intention whatsoever to bash anyone and, of all the people, not the ministers of the Gospel. But hypocrites, like the Pharisees of the Lord's time, constitute danger to the body of Christ and must not be tolerated or encouraged. I am writing as one prompted by the Spirit of God and out of true personal experience of the prevailing truth relative to most churches and ministers today. In some parts of the world, the competition among the ministers is so fierce and deadly that there are churches on every corner; and it is not strange to have more than four churches in one building, all holding their services on the same days and at the same times. I had occasions to minister in churches in which it was almost impossible to hear myself because the other churches next door had their bands and mega loud speakers so high, with the obvious intention to drown the activities of the other competing small churches. So intentional, insensitive, and with absurd reckless and malicious disregard to the rights of others and fear of God. Some have engaged, and still engage, in designing and desiring the fall of other ministers; some laugh at the calamity of others, and some build their empires around them and their families and abhor giving any chance or opportunity to another except a member of their family to excel. This kind of envy, hatred, selfishness, division, and strife are common destructive trends to the body of Christ. As we have already read, if the body of Christ continues to bite and devour itself, it will one day consume itself (see Gal 5:15). If we are led by the Spirit of God, we shall have one spiritual mind (the mind of Christ), and there should be no room to fulfill the lusts of the flesh. Where there is no peace, the Spirit of God is not there, for God cannot be associated with strife and division. "For God is not the author of confusion but of peace, as in all the churches of the saints" (1 Cor 14:33). The disciple James was blunt and direct and to the point about this issue "But if you have bitter envy and self-seeking in your hearts, do not boast and lie against the truth. This wisdom does not descend from above, but is earthly, sensual, demonic. For where envy and self-seeking exist, confusion and every evil thing are there" (Jas 3:14-16).

Sometimes, the church leadership brings about strife and division and internal squabbles to themselves when they act carnally in the selection of board members, elders, deacons, and other church officials. Most churches have the so-called known names and moneybags in their leadership roster. These people are chosen not because of any spiritual calling on their lives or faithfulness, but simply because of their ability—real or perceived. And no sooner there arises any conflict or disagreement; the able person will put his ability to work in splitting the church. While an able man may not be faithful, a faithful man, on the other hand, can be both. A faithful person is a gift from God. "Moreover it is required in stewards that one be found faithful" (1 Cor 4:2).

Again, the apostle Paul admonished Timothy thus, "And the things that you have heard from me among many witnesses, commit these to faithful men who will be able to teach others also" (2 Tm 2:2). The book of Proverbs did not mince any words in describing an unfaithful person. "Confidence in an unfaithful man in time of trouble is like a bad tooth and a foot out of joint" (Prv 25:19). Therefore, it is better to have the poorest faithful person than an unfaithful billionaire. It is the heart of a person that God searches.

Sadly, there are some mischievous members of church congregations that the leadership of the church must certainly deal with. These are the "know it all" members who hold themselves out as higher than all others, boasting and puffing up. They think and convince themselves that they have the only good ideas; they are proud and devoid of humility. They will stop at nothing to ensure torment, trouble, discord, and confusion. They strive in devilish arena (to steal, kill, and destroy). And when they decide to leave a particular church, they will not be satisfied to leave quietly and alone but would rather take others along with them. They will make sure they pull down whatever they assisted in building. They love to boast that they were the pillars of the church, and as soon as they left, the church fell apart. They fail to realize that whoever pulls down what he has helped to build is a transgressor; and whosoever refuses to leave alone but makes conscious efforts to pull people away with him is of the devil. It is one thing for anyone to leave a church for any cause at all; it is another to form a rebellious mutiny against a church. So as you gather in His name, examine carefully if you are gathering together in agreement in His name or against Him. We cannot please God when we are in disagreement with Him.

The topic discussed above is well illustrated in the book of Isaiah 58, in response to the people's complaint that the Lord ignored them even when they fasted and gathered together in His name. The Lord said, among others, "Indeed you fast for strife and debate, and to strike with the fist of wickedness.

You will not fast as you do this day, to make your voice heard on high. Is it a fast that I have chosen, a day for a man to afflict his soul? Is it to bow down his head like a bulrush, and to spread out sackcloth and ashes? Would you call this a fast, and an acceptable day to the Lord?. Is this not the fast that I have chosen: To loose the bonds of wickedness, to undo the heavy burdens, to let the oppressed go free, and that you break every yoke?" (Is 58:4-6). That is truly gathering together in His name.

Chapter Ten

THE FOUNDATION OF SPIRITUAL FORGIVENESS FOR OTHERS

Love is to God as forgiveness is to love. Therefore, God is perfect love and forgiveness. One who says he loves God but forgives not others is a liar and a hypocrite. There is indeed a direct relationship between love and forgiveness. Sadly, the most unforgiving hearts are among those of us who profess to be strong Christians. Some of us would say they love the one who has hurt them badly but will never forgive and forget the offender and the offense. They would even stop speaking to the offender as long as they live. Many of us have neither spoken to nor have anything to do with either parent or both parents and their siblings for many years. Imagine eating yourself up in bitterness and anguish of unforgiveness for so long. Now imagine this, if the Lord comes this moment and you are caught up in such evil and unforgiving heart, what will be your fate? For it is written that only those who are pure in heart shall see God (see Mt 5:8). A bitter and unforgiving heart cannot be said to be pure—unforgiveness being sinful and the worst form of witchcraft. A heart that finds it hard to forgive is not a heart of the flesh and not of God. It is this newly given spiritual heart that makes one who is born of God a new creature, with a heart of God. This is a heart of love, compassion, mercy, grace, peace, meekness, gentleness, forgiveness, and reconciliation. It is not a hardened and stubborn heart (heart of stone), but a peculiar spiritual heart that is capable of loving and forgiving even the worst enemies.

Sadly, most of us are heavily influenced by our various cultures in this regard. In developing nations, like Africa for example, it is culturally and traditionally unacceptable to keep grudges against relatives, friends, and neighbors for long without approaching them with your grievances, with the most sincere hope of resolving the matter quickly. It is even considered an abomination to switch off communication with parents and siblings—what with the complex nature of the extended family system, where everyone's business is another's business, and one life is the responsibility of all. Hence the common saying that it takes a village to raise a child (much similar to the doctrine of Christ-bearing one another's burden). In these cultures, which are unfortunately referred in some quarters as primitive, the conceptual baggage of individualism is properly viewed as not in keeping with the reality of life and therefore inconsistent with God's plans for humans. Perhaps we should borrow a loving and forgiving leaf from dogs, which, even when they are hurt or punished, forgive and reconcile easily from the heart and even respond to the master with love. The argument, of course, may be that humans are so complex that it is not possible for them to love and forgive as dogs. But we are not here talking about ordinary people; rather, we are talking about Christians—Christ-like beings, those new creatures who are born of God (the given elect of God), with new hearts

The Foundation Of Spiritual Forgiveness For Others

of flesh, spiritual mind, body, and new spirit. These are those given the power to become children of God, plucked from a refining fire, the gods on earth, who have put on Christ and do the works of Christ (see Jn 1:12, 14:12; Gal 3:37). They are the light and salt of the world and, as such, operate within the culture, tradition, and doctrine of the truth of the Gospel of Jesus Christ, our Lord.

Forgiveness of others is a pardon for all their wrong deeds. It is a total release from and discharge of all debts. It is simply an act of setting an offender free from the yoke of our bitterness, resentment, and hatred. However, on the other hand, spiritual forgiveness is such pardon or discharge that leaves no trace or residual bitterness in our heart. It is an act that sets both the offended and the offender free from bondage. Spiritual forgiveness is not only one of the highest levels of divine maturity; it is a profound fruit of the Holy Spirit. There may not be found up to 1 percent of us who possess and practice true spiritual forgiveness. The spiritual forgiveness from the heart for others as commanded by God is a total liberation from the heart.

A beautiful illustration is that which has been cited by many about a prisoner who is fined and imprisoned until he pays a heavy fine. Unable to pay his way out of prison, he resolves to surrender to total hopelessness. Suddenly, a good person he has never known comes along and pays off the debt, and he is set free without strings attached. Our poor prisoner gets out totally forgiven, discharged, released, and set free, for all the debts are paid. That was what our Lord did for those who believe in Him. My addition to that illustration is that when our prisoner walks out a free man, he inquires of the good man who paid his debts, but no one knows his whereabouts, except he left a note for the freed prisoner, which reads, "As I have forgiven and showed you love, do likewise to others."

THE LORD'S DEMONSTRATION

Our Lord and Savior, Jesus Christ, demonstrated spiritual forgiveness in three specific instances: (a) Responding to the woman caught in adultery, the Lord forgave her without condemnation, but rather pointed her to the way of salvation (go and sin no more) (see Jn 8:11). We must take note that the woman in this case sinned against God; (b) While on the cross, being crucified, he forgave from the heart and prayed the Father to forgive all, "Father, forgive them, for they do not know what they do" (Lk 23:34); (c) In dealing with Apostle Paul (then Saul) on his way to Damascus to persecute His disciples and church, the Lord not only forgave Paul, but He also graciously told him what to do to obtain life (salvation). "Arise and go into the city, and you will be told what you must do" (Acts 9:6).

In the three cases above, our Lord demonstrated two significant things:

a. *His only mission: to seek and save the lost.* And as the light of the world, He would teach and impart knowledge to the ignorant, show the way to the lost, and heal the sick. By so doing, He fulfilled the prophecies of His mission (see Is 66:1-2) and glorified the Father's name by doing the good works of His Father. The salvation of a lost soul brings God joy and glory. As we have read, God despairs over the death of a sinner; it is not His pleasure that anyone should perish (see Ez 18:23). That is why

The Foundation Of Spiritual Forgiveness For Others

there is joyful celebration in heaven for one saved soul. "I say to you that likewise there will be more joy in heaven over one sinner who repents than over ninety-nine just persons who need no repentance" (Lk 15:7). The mission of our Lord is the same mission for those who believe in Him; hence, He has commissioned us to carry His mission to the end (see Mt 28:19-20). Again, as He clearly stated, "Most assuredly, I say to you, he who believes in Me, the works that I do he will do also; and greater works than these he will do, because I go to My Father" (Jn 14:12).

b. *We cannot win a soul for the kingdom of God through hatred, resentment, unforgiveness, judgment, and condemnation but rather through love, compassion, forgiveness, mercy, and grace.* It is certainly obvious that the people we hate, judge, condemn, and bear grudges against stay far away from us. They fear us because we exhibit imperfect love by our works. But as a light of Christ in the world, we ought to let it shine so that people may see the good works we do in Christ's name and glorify our Father (see Mt 5:16). But if what we do runs contrary to the mission of the Lord, we are none of His.

So then, there is a new commandment to those who are of Christ, which commandment is not really new: forgive others (all) as Christ has forgiven us. By such Christ-like works, the world may know we are truly of Christ. For we have been forgiven and saved by grace, so it is incumbent on us to extend that same grace to everyone, no matter how they hurt us; otherwise, we become ungrateful and wicked children. "And be kind to one another, tenderhearted, forgiving one another, even as God in Christ forgave you" (Eph 4:32). "Bearing with one another, and forgiving one another, if anyone has a complaint against another; even as Christ forgave you, so you also must do. But above all these things put on love, which is the bond of perfection" (Col 3:13-14).

HOW TO FORGIVE

Since unforgiveness is sin, we must begin our walk of spiritual forgiveness from point number 1—*us*. We must ask the Lord to forgive us for any trace of unforgiveness in our heart, pray and confess our absolute forgiveness of any and all those we harbor unforgiveness and resentment against, ask God to give us a new spiritual heart and a new spirit from then on, and pray to God to forgive and deliver us and the offenders from the domain of darkness.

WHOM DO YOU FORGIVE?

We must forgive from the heart any and all persons who have wronged us at any time. "And whenever you stand praying, if you have anything against anyone, forgive him, that your Father in heaven may also forgive you your trespasses" (Mk 11:25).

HOW OFTEN?

Asked by apostle Peter how often he should forgive his brother, the Lord answered him thus, "I do not say to you, up to seven times, but up to seventy times seven" (Mt 18:22). In other words, we are to forgive all, all the time. There is therefore no limit to forgiveness as there is no limit to love.

SOME CONSEQUENCES OF UNFORGIVENESS

Unforgiveness has both spiritual and physical serious consequences, which include, but are not limited to, the following:

a. *Hinders God's forgiveness.* As obvious and elementary this may sound, but how many of us commit this to heart? There is complete nonchalant attitude toward this most serious consequence of unforgiveness. The commandment to forgive others is a commandment with a promise. If we forgive, we will be forgiven by God (see Mt 6:14-15). If, however, we refuse to forgive others no matter what the justification may be, God will not forgive us. Simple and fair enough. Whoever seeks forgiveness from God must come with clean hands (heart). Just as whoever seeks equity must do equity. While speaking on this point in Africa, the Lord asked the congregation why they imputed curse on themselves daily. As you can imagine, there was a big stir, and the Lord told me to ask the congregation to recite the Lord's Prayer. As the recital was going on, the Lord halted it when they got to the Gospel of Matthew 6:12. "And forgive us our debts as we forgive our debtors." "STOP," said the Lord, "So be it according to your words, and I will not forgive because you do not forgive others." "You therefore pronounce a curse on yourselves all the time."

b. *Hinders prayers.* When we pray to God with unforgiveness in our heart, He will not hear us just as it was with Joshua, the high priest in the book of Zechariah 3, who was standing before an angel of the Lord but was being withheld by Satan because he had filthy garments on. Satan, the accuser, continued to withhold Joshua until the filthy garments on him were removed. "Then He showed me Joshua the high priest standing before the Angel of the Lord, and Satan standing at his right hand to oppose him" (Zec 3:1). And the Lord said to Satan, "The Lord rebuke you, Satan! The Lord who has chosen Jerusalem rebuke you! Is this not a brand plucked from the fire?" (Zec 3:2). Although the high priest Joshua was one plucked out of the fire, Satan resisted him because "now Joshua was clothed with filthy garments, and was standing before the Angel" (Zec 3:3). Then the Lord ordered that the filthy garments be removed first. Then He answered and spoke to those who stood before him, saying, "Take away the filthy garments from him." And to him, He said, "See, I have removed your iniquity from you, and I will clothe you with rich robes" (Zec 3:4). Spiritually, the filthy garments the Lord was referring to were not mere physical clothes but the condition of the heart. As the psalmist rightly says, God will not hear us if we have iniquity in our heart (see Ps 66:18). And that is consistent with the word of the Lord: "Therefore if you bring your gift to the altar, and there remember that your brother has something against you, leave your gift there before the altar, and go your way. First be reconciled to your brother, and then come and offer your gift" (Mt 5:23-24).

The Foundation Of Spiritual Forgiveness For Others

c. *Grieves the Holy Spirit daily.* An unforgiving heart is for all purposes a wicked heart. The Holy Spirit cannot dwell in a blemished house because an impure and wicked heart grieves Him. An unforgiving heart is therefore a breeding ground for evil works. It was due to the wickedness of man that grieved God so much that He regretted creating man, which led subsequently to the destruction of the first world (see Gn 6:5-6). Referring to the rebellious and wicked works of God's people, the prophet Isaiah wrote, "But they rebelled and grieved His Holy Spirit; so He turned Himself against them as an enemy, and He fought against them" (63:10). As we have already read, God is daily angry with a wicked heart (see Ps 7:11). Therefore, as a proper admonishment, we shall not give room whereby the Holy Spirit is grieved. "And do not grieve the Holy Spirit of God, by whom you were sealed for the day of redemption." (Eph 4:30).

d. *Puts you and the offender in perpetual bondage.* Unforgiveness is a deadly form of witchcraft that eats up both the offender and the offended. Now imagine what happens to your nerves and spirit when you come face-to-face with the one you have not forgiven. Even the mere thought of him or the mention of his name makes your blood boil to your detriment. Even merely seeing or hearing the sound of what belongs to him turns your stomach the wrong way. And pray to God that you do not remember your unforgiven enemies right before you retire for the night. The more unforgiveness remains in our heart, the more hardened our heart is. And in truth, to a greater extent, the unforgiving heart is anguished more than the offender's, who sometimes does not realize the torment that the unforgiving heart is subjected to. While the unforgiving heart may spend all night agonizing and eating himself up, the offender may be enjoying his good night's sleep.

e. *Hinders spiritual healing, and liberty.* No matter how hard we try, we cannot obtain complete spiritual healing, liberty, and maturity, where there is a trace of unforgiveness in our heart. For where the spirit of the Lord is not, there is no liberty. Therefore, an unforgiving heart cannot be free.

f. *Promotes physical ailment.* As stated above, unforgiveness is as a sin of witchcraft that eats both the offender and the offended. An unforgiving heart has no peace. The resentment, anger, and bitterness resulting from unforgiveness promote stress, depression, headaches, heartache, anxiety, and many other ailments. Therefore, unforgiveness kills both the spirit and the flesh. It is a very deadly poison.

g. *Leads to temptation.* Unforgiveness is a spiritual weak point, which gives the devil easy access to tempt us. It is an invitation to the devil to explore our weakness to the fullest. As we pray to God not to lead us into temptation, we ought not to lead ourselves into temptation (see Mt 6:13).

Chapter Eleven

THE TRUE SPIRITUAL FORGIVENESS

This profound fruit of the Holy Spirit is forgiveness from a spiritual heart that is poured out to the offender in love and sees him as one who is perished and needs knowledge of God. As gods, those who are born of God must forgive completely from a heart of God; our heart and mouth must necessarily be in harmony.

FORGIVE AND FORGET

Forgiveness is not spiritually effective unless we forgive and forget. Those who are born of God are spirits of God and gods to unbelievers and, therefore, must be perfect in love and forgiveness as God is. "No more shall every man teach his neighbor, and every man his brother, saying, 'Know the Lord,' for they all shall know Me, from the least of them to the greatest of them, says the Lord. For I will forgive their iniquity, and their sin I will remember no more" (Jer 31:34). "I, even I, am He who blots out your transgressions for My own sake; and I will not remember your sins" (Is 43:25). But can any person forgive and forget the evil perpetuated against him or her? After all, we are humans, and ugly memories cannot easily be erased. The answer I usually get from congregations is *no*. It is indeed almost impossible to forgive and forget who and what hurts you so much. If we profess forgiveness but each time we see or remember the offender we become angry, bitter, and resentful, have we truly forgiven that person? We have not. But if and when we remember the offender and/or the evil deed, our hearts glorify God for His mercy and how He used the incident to teach us, then the Spirit of God indeed dwells in us. For no evil can happen to one born of God unless God allows it. If we are consumed by unforgiveness and resentment, or negative feelings, we will not appreciate what God has planned for us to become as a result thereof. This is not to say we may not remember the forgiven past, but if we remember it, it is manifested as a testimony of glory and thanksgiving to God; then we have entered a higher or more perfect understanding of the mysteries of the kingdom of God. But if and when we remember, and our hearts have no trace of hatred and bitterness but instead, mercy, grace, compassion, and love toward the offender are found, then in truth, we have become gods and perfect in love as our heavenly Father is (see Mt 5:48).

A walk in the spirit is not about what we have accomplished or the affliction, persecution, or hurt we have suffered but rather it is what we have become as a result. Did we pass the test for the next promotion, or must we, to the extent is necessary, repeat the lesson? The critical element in this regard is our spiritual attitude toward affliction, tribulation, wickedness, etc. Spiritual attitude or the spiritual eye of things happening to us determines the level of pain and victory or defeat. If we, from the heart, accept every affliction/evil as a blessing, an opportunity to overcome the wicked one to God's glory, victory will always be ours in the end. Now, this is our victory if we endure to the end without offending God. Otherwise, we assume wrongly that we have simply won the battle because we managed to squeeze or scheme ourselves out of the difficulty, but in actuality, we lost the war by offending God in the process. As with many of us, I too have testimonies of evil deeds against me, which I now regard as blessings. One thing we do not seem to comprehend is that sometimes God allows evil things in our lives to get us to His expected end. Some brief examples are in order:

a. *Joseph, Son of Jacob.* His afflictions were designed to save Israel from death. Hear his response to the worst betrayal by his siblings: "But as for you, you meant evil against me; but God meant it for good, in order to bring it about as it is this day, to save many people alive" (Gn 50:20).
b. *Jesus Christ.* The calculated evil was to destroy the Lord; and for His mother, brethren, and disciples, it was a devastating blow far beyond our wildest imaginations. But God allowed it for the greater good, the salvation of all who believe.
c. *Paul (known as Saul).* Saul, the legendary apostle and servant of Jesus, was wrecking havoc against believers, yet God allowed him until the appointed time. Why? Saul's persecution was a spiritual tool on the part of God to spread the Gospel to many other parts beyond the confines of Jerusalem. As Saul intensified his persecution, the disciples who were afraid to venture outside the comfort zone of Jerusalem had no choice but to escape to other cities, and there they preached the Gospel. "As for Saul, he made havoc of the church,

entering every house, and dragging off men and women, committing them to prison. Therefore those who were scattered went everywhere preaching the word" (Acts 8:3-4). I am mindful of some readers who may still not fully comprehend this point, but we all agree that with the Spirit of God, all things are possible and that all things work together for good to them who are of God (see Mt 19:26; Rom 8:28). All Christians should therefore pray for this profound fruit of the Holy Spirit (spiritual forgiveness) for their own good.

THE MYSTERY OF SPIRITUAL FORGIVENESS

Does God retract His forgiveness once He has forgiven a sinner? Put another way, when God has forgiven a sinner today, can He, at a later date—say, one month subsequent—retract the forgiveness? That was the question the Lord asked me during my recent stay in Africa. My answer and the answer given by every congregation which I had posed the same question to was a resounding *no*. That may be your answer too. Once God has forgiven us, He has forgiven, period. Right? No, we are all wrong, not comprehending the mysteries of the kingdom of God. The Lord told me that I was wrong, that He would retract His forgiveness when the one He has forgiven hardens his heart and refuses to forgive another. *Wow!* What a devastating consequence of unforgiveness. In the Gospel of Matthew 18, our Lord gave a parable of an unforgiving servant whose master forgave so large a debt but who refused to forgive a fellow servant of a small debt owed him. As the master mercifully obliged the ungrateful servant's pleas for forgiveness, he (the unforgiving servant) ought to have done the same to a fellow servant. But he would have none of it. Rather, he committed his fellow servant to prison until he could pay the debt. When his master heard what his wicked servant did, he was wroth and said to him, "Then his master, after he had called him, said to him, 'You wicked servant! I forgave you all that debt because you begged me. Should you not also have had compassion on your fellow servant, just as I had pity on you?'" (Mt 18:32-33). And then the master who forgave him previously changed his mind and retracted his forgiveness and committed the wicked servant to prison until he paid the debt. The Lord then said, "So My heavenly Father also will do to you if each of you, from his heart, does not forgive his brother his trespasses" (Mt 18:35). It is certainly true that most of us have read these scriptures many times without the understanding of the revelation of the mystery surrounding spiritual forgiveness. For it is written, "For with what judgment you judge, you will be judged; and with the measure you use, it will be measured back to you" (Mt 7:2). Those who have ears of the heart to hear, let them hear.

Chapter Twelve

THE FOUNDATION OF SPIRITUAL RECONCILIATION

Forgiveness is to love as reconciliation is to forgiveness. Therefore, love is forgiveness and reconciliation as God is love. Reconciliation is the act of bringing together that which is apart, or kept apart or separated, but which, for all purposes, ought to be one. It is the restoration or harmonization of soured relationship. The specific mission of our Lord and Savior, Jesus Christ, was to reconcile man with his Creator. As a result of the fall of Adam, humans who were originally created in God's image and likeness (one with God) became separated and apart from Him, hence the necessity for a Divine Reconciler, Advocate, Redeemer, and Messiah.

RECONCILIATION WITH GOD

As discussed in previous chapters, we cannot be one with God unless there is spiritual agreement. Desirous of this intimate relationship, God manifests His ultimate love for us

The Foundation Of Spiritual Reconciliation

by sacrificing His only son, offering Him as atonement for our sins. "But God demonstrates His own love towards us, in that while we were still sinners, Christ died for us. For if when we were enemies we were reconciled to God through the death of His son. And not only that, but we also rejoice in God through our Lord Jesus Christ, through whom we have now received the atonement [reconciliation]" (Rom 5:8, 10-11).

As a reconciler, the desire and mission of our Lord was to first reconcile all to Himself and to God through Him. It is worthy of note that God loved us so much, and as a demonstration of this perfect love, He did not hold back reconciliation until we repented (see Jn 3:16; Rom 5:8, 10). As a necessity and practical matter, the Lord first had to reconcile us to Himself—a classic demonstration that charity begins at home; and one cannot give what he or she does not have. Therefore, the coming of the Lord was to reconcile us to the Father through Him, thereby giving us an example to follow. Our Lord came down from heaven to show us the way to the Father; for He is the way, a highway of righteousness and holiness to those who believe (see Is 35:8). And those who believe in Him must necessarily do His works (see Jn 14:12). If then we are one with Christ, we should work within the scope of His commission. Our mission then should be to reconcile all people to Christ through us to the glory of the Father.

Spiritual reconciliation to God is a total fusing together with God (one with Him) through Jesus Christ by way of the two spiritual foundations of repentance and agreement, anchored on the two keys to the kingdom of God—love and obedience. Again, this is being born of God.

RECONCILIATION WITH OTHERS

As it is with the love for others, the greater difficulty lies in reconciliation with others. Yet there cannot be spiritual reconciliation between God and man devoid of reconciliation between man and man. If we cannot reconcile with the one we see, how can we reconcile with God, who is Spirit? In this regard, most of us are found vain, lacking, and hypocritical. We proudly profess and even believe we are holy angels of the Lord, yet we have people locked up in our convenient delete mode—people we have sworn not to speak to as long as we live, yet we do not know how long we will live. Some of us will rather carry on daily conversations with animals and plants. Oh, how screwed up is the priority of humans. If we love and reconcile with others as Christ has done for us, then we are His disciples, doing His works and keeping His commandments. As with Christ, the mission of His true disciples is twofold: (a) reconcile with others and (b) reconcile others with Jesus. This is knowing God and making Him known throughout the earth. This is the mandate of Jesus to His disciples: "Go therefore and make disciples of all the nations, baptizing them in the name of the Father, and of the Son, and of the Holy Spirit, teaching them to observe all things that I have commanded you" (Mt 28:19-20).

Anyone who professes to be born of God, or claims he knows God, and there remains one individual he has neither forgiven nor reconciled with, or attempted in all godly sincerity and good conscience to reconcile with, deceives himself. For yet the individual walks in darkness, clothed in filthy garments (see 1 Jn 1:5-6; Zech 3:1-3). For how can we reconcile others with Christ when we ourselves are not yet reconciled within

The Foundation Of Spiritual Reconciliation

us? For us who preach reconciliation, are we unable to reconcile ourselves? We must live the word of God, which we profess, and not say one thing and do another. Jesus Christ is not only the greatest spiritual reconciler of man to God but also man to man.

Wherever Jesus Christ enters, or His name is truly observed, there must, of necessity, be love, peace, calm, reconciliation, and liberty (the captive set free). "The Spirit of the Lord God is upon Me, because the Lord has anointed Me to preach good tidings to the poor; He has sent Me to heal the brokenhearted, to proclaim liberty to the captives, and the opening of the prison to those who are bound" (Is 61:1). Most of us read the above scripture without spiritual understanding. We fail to consider those held captive and imprisoned within the walls of our irreconcilable hardened hearts. As a result of such misunderstanding, some go about seeking to minister to only those who are physically incarcerated, taking no thought about those spiritually incarcerated in their hearts, thereby rendering themselves spiritually ineffective. Charity, they say, begins at home. If the Spirit of God is upon us, we should begin today by reconciling with all, thereby setting all who have hurt us free from captivity, as Christ, our Lord, did for us. As it is written, "Pursue peace with all people, and holiness, without which no one will see the Lord" (Heb 12:14) (see also Ps 34:14). The presence of our Lord and Savior, Jesus Christ, makes all things new (see Rev 21:5). The scriptures tell us that Pontius Pilate and King Herod, who were previously enemies, reconciled the very day Jesus was brought to their presence, though separately. "That very day Pilate and Herod became friends with each other, for previously they had been at enmity with each other" (Lk 23:12).

Reconciliation is therefore the completeness of true forgiveness of others. If then we profess that Christ is in us and there remains an ugly past within us that forecloses forgiveness and reconciliation, we deceive ourselves. Reconciliation to others and others to Christ through us is a commandment of the Lord and, therefore, our mission and ministry. "Now all things are of God, who has reconciled us to Himself through Jesus Christ, and has given us the ministry of reconciliation, that is, that God was in Christ reconciling the world to Himself, not imputing their trespasses to them, and has committed to us the word of reconciliation" (2 Cor 5:18-19). We cannot reconcile with Christ that individual who knows we hate or resent him. As a matter of fact, the ungodly example (works) we exhibit by way of bitterness and resentment will only lead the unbeliever to resent the God we serve. For it is by way of good works we do in the name of the Lord that people see and glorify the name of God (see Mt 5:16; 1 Pt 2:12). Therefore, at the same token, our bad works glorify the devil and displease God (see Rom 2:23-24).

The most important consequence of irreconcilability is the hindrance of prayers and spiritual growth (see Mt 5:23-24). We cannot bear good fruits for the kingdom of God when we are burdened by the spirit of irreconcilability. As we know, a bad tree cannot produce good fruits.

The one common question I have been confronted with is what to do with an unrepentant soul, or one who refuses to reconcile. As stated earlier, a born of God must reconcile or attempt, in all godly sincerity and good conscience, to reconcile with all. God watches and sees our hearts, even the most hidden parts. Whatever it takes to ensure the sanctification and purification of the heart in accordance with the grace given to us

The Foundation Of Spiritual Reconciliation

must be done. The kingdom of God is now nearer at hand than ever before; it therefore behooves all those who have hope in God to purify themselves as He is pure (see 1 Jn 3:3). "Therefore, having these promises, beloved, let us cleanse ourselves from all filthiness of the flesh and spirit, perfecting holiness in the fear of God" (2 Cor 7:1). You may be snubbed, and if you are told to take a hike, so be it; as long as your heart is now pure from lingering bitterness and resentment, it is well with you. However, from then on, your spiritual assignment is ushered in as you are under spiritual obligation to intercede and pray to God for the stubborn heart. Here, our love and compassion are tested. Do we react to the offender's snub with the same measure, or do we show mercy and love for one who lacks knowledge of God? It is godly not to be the fool of the world but for the kingdom.

Now, what of the brother or sister who shows no remorse whatsoever, unwilling to ask for forgiveness and, in most cases, taunting you and adding insult to injury? This individual lacks knowledge, and therefore he is lost. You who are the light of the world, with spiritual heart and mind of Christ, should, by your good works, teach and show him the right way. It is spiritually prudent not to wait for the offending individual to come to you, for he may not come, seeing that he is full of pride and hardened heart; rather, forgive him by showing him love and compassion as Christ showed us. When the Lord was being crucified, he forgave his tormentors without conditions and reservations. Most people who are spiritually lost and sick may never bring themselves to ask for forgiveness. We must be prepared to demonstrate from our hearts what differentiates and separates us from them. That was what the father of the prodigal son did, as well as the owner of the one lost sheep. They both sought for the lost and not the other way around.

And the Lord commanded us to love our enemies, for such heart and spirit differentiate us from those who do not know God (see Mt 5:45). Most of us will go after a stubborn lost pet each time it strays or runs away, even as many times as the animal rebels, yet we cannot do the same for a human being who is created in the image of God. So what is a pet more to us than a brother or sister?

What if we are not so sure who is actually the offender, and yet a sour relationship has taken an ugly center stage? For avoidance of any doubt (sin) and to free your conscience and soul, be the example and take the bold step as the fool for the kingdom of God and seek to reconcile even if you must condescend to say you are sorry—no matter who is at fault. You must seek and attempt, in all godly sincerity, to reconcile immediately, especially in a situation when you have offended someone or you are not so sure who is at fault. Act as the one at fault and let God be the judge. The longer a matter remains unresolved, the harder to condescend in humility and the hardened the heart becomes. If you do not immediately wash your hands after eating a sticky food with them, they harden with time. And of course, the longer the hands remain dirty, the harder to clean the mess. It is a lot easier to uproot a tender young tree than a mature and strong one. The advantage of early intervention cannot be overemphasized. In every situation, when you become a fool for the kingdom of God's sake, you disarm the evil one. Perhaps this lends clearer understanding to the commandment of the Lord that we should not resist an evil person (see Mt 5:39). It is life to quickly cut off the devil's expectations in an ugly and trying situation. As is written, "Agree with your adversary quickly, while you are on the way with him, lest your adversary deliver you to the judge, the judge hand you over to the officer, and you be thrown into prison" (Mt 5:25). How then do we, as disciples of Jesus Christ, bless any home or person with peace if we lack peace in us?

And by the way, I ask you to heed this advice: do not qualify your *sorry* with *but*. For example, "I am sorry, but . . ." *But* negates remorsefulness and only engenders argument and defensiveness. It means that you are qualifying your peace initiative, and you may not be really sorry; but you are just saying so out of obligation rather than love and reverence to God. Being argumentative and defensive exposes the pride in us and gives room to the devil to exploit the situation.

How do we reconcile with those we have lost contact with and do not know their whereabouts? The true reconciliation is in the heart, and God watches and sees our hearts. If we forgive and reconcile fully in our heart as a demonstration of true love and reconciliation and keep our enemies in prayers and good thoughts, we have, indeed, reconciled with them.

But this is not in conformity with the daily reality of this world, some may say. And who can do it? I respectfully agree that no human being can do this except when he is born of God and given by the Spirit of reconciliation—the Spirit of Jesus Christ. This is that peculiar person who is born of the Spirit of God, transformed into the image of Christ, given the power to become a child of God, and is led by His Spirit. That is the person who now can do all things through Christ who strengthens him, for we know that with the Spirit of God, *all things are possible.*

OBEDIENCE:
THE SECOND KEY TO
THE KINGDOM OF GOD

Chapter Thirteen

OBEDIENCE (OBEY)

God is all about love and obedience—the two inseparable keys to His kingdom. As such, by extension, one who is born of God is born into perfect love and obedience—the whole duty of man. Therefore, the whole duty of man is to live the two keys to the kingdom of God—love and obey. Love God with all your being, love others as God loves you, and implicitly obey all God's commandments. The first and the second keys are one, and none can exist independent of the other. Where there is no obedience, there is no love, and verse versa.

The intensity of one's love of God is proportionately reflected in the level of his obedience to God's words. The only way to manifest our love of God is to obey all His commandments (see Jn 14:15). Revising that statement, we can conclude with substantial authority that those who hate God disobey Him. Now this may sound very extreme, judgmental, and condemning; nevertheless, it is biblical. Our Lord said that those who do not love Him disobey His commandments. "He who does not love Me does not keep My words" (Jn 14:24). Again, the Lord cautioned that those who are not with Him are against Him. As says the scripture, "You are My friends if you do whatever I command you" (Jn 15:14).

It is therefore not what we say but what we do that show that Jesus Christ is our lord and master. The world will identify us as children of God and disciples of Jesus Christ if we do the works of God through obedience to His words. That is the same pattern of love that exists between the Son and the Father. "But that the world may know that I love the Father, and as the Father gave Me commandments, so I do" (Jn 14:31).

So whomever we do our works for is the one we love, and the one we love, we obey, and as the Lord has warned, we cannot serve two masters—one leg in the church and the other leg in the world or one person wearing two different hats and faces.

The only way to know, thank, appreciate, live, serve, and please God is to obey Him. There is, of course, a difference between knowing of God and knowing God. While just about every person on this planet seems to know and hear of God and can even mention His name either in praise or blasphemy, those who truly know God are those who obey Him. "Now by this we know that we know Him, if we keep His commandments. He who says I know Him and does not keep His commandants, is a liar, and the truth is not in him" (1 Jn 2:3-4). Without implicit obedience to the words of God, every other thing we do, be it the sacrificing of our bodies or living daily in churches, is in vain. "Behold, to obey is better than sacrifice" (1 Sm 15:22). The ultimate sacrifice was made on the cross in obedience unto death. The only sacrifice left is a contrite, broken, submissive, humble, and obedient heart.

HOW TO OBEY GOD

Since the only sacrifice acceptable to God is a broken heart, obedience is only effective when coming from a humble heart. God abhors those who pretend to worship and obey Him with their mouths while their hearts are far away from Him. These are hypocrites whose hearts are in disagreement with their mouths. These people talk and profess much but do nothing or very little. They are hearers but not doers of what they hear. During the days of my house confinement, the Lord commanded me to live whatever He taught me and teach others exactly the same. I cried for days in prayers and supplications asking for His grace to live His words. Next, the Lord told me to never obey Him out of fear or obligation, but rather out of love for Him and reverence to His name. Since those born of God are led by His Spirit and therefore children of God (gods), obedience to God should be first nature to them, without deliberations and even conscious thoughts. Because God lives in them and they live God, they are one with God. It is like taking a cup of water, which has become part of our lives; there are no more prior conscious thoughts of how to drink and swallow that water. This is tantamount to the spiritual walk of those who are truly born of God. Although they fear God, they do not do things out of fear. To fear God is to depart (forsake) evil (see Prv 8:13)—while doing things out of fear is the manifestation of imperfect love, lack of total spiritual agreement with God, and at best, obligatory (eye service). Humans can hide their thoughts and deceive one another, but can any deceive God?

It is rather difficult to explain the spirit-filled life. It is the Spirit of God that quickens God's children to walk in sprit and do all things through Christ, our Lord. Explaining this concept to Nicodemus, the Lord answered thus, "The wind blows where it wishes, and you hear the sound of it, but cannot tell where it comes from, and where it goes, so is everyone who is born of the Spirit" (Jn 3:8).

I have always posed this hypothetical scenario and question to congregations relative to this matter. While shopping, I see a beautiful item and take it, leave the store, and drive off; two minutes later, being convicted and fearful of God, I turn back and restore the item and finally leave satisfied. The question is, have I stolen? The answer I usually get is no. But in truth, before God, I have stolen. If I am born of God and fear Him, I would not have done what I did in the first place. You see, I only returned the item out of fear and obligation, but God saw my heart from the beginning. The Lord's teaching is in harmony with the above conclusion. He clarifies that adultery, for example, occurs first in the heart. "But I say to you that whoever looks at a woman to lust for her has already committed adultery with her in his heart" (Mt 5:28). A polluted heart is not God's acceptable sacrifice.

Second, we are commanded to obey all of God's commandments or words. It is an all-or-nothing relationship. There is no middle ground, no room for selective obedience, and no condition precedent to obedience. Therefore, we cannot pick and choose which of God's commandments, or words, we should obey. "For whoever shall keep the whole law, and yet stumble in one point, he is guilty of all" (Jas 2:10).

Our God is the God of "if." If we do our part according to His rules and procedure, He does the part He has promised, and He is a covenant-keeping God. These days, unlike the servants of God of the old, we are consumed by what we want God to do for us, but unwilling to live strictly according to His will. God has His established way; it is either His way or the highway to hell. Amazingly, some of us even demand or order God around in *prayers* to grant our heart's desires—"if you are my God . . ." What a terrible way of provoking God. What if God would say, "Very well then, so be it, I am not your God"? What would we do? We are indeed a generation of immediate gratification: "We want it now, you hear me, God. Now click the button, and it is done." If not, it will seem as if the end has come.

I had an opportunity of counseling a couple who were having some marital and other difficulties. Apparently, they had had some lingering problems for over ten years, living under the same roof—in hell, I dare to say—succeeding falsely to put out good faces to outsiders, professing to have been born again for over fifteen years. While dealing with an issue, I appropriately reminded them of their respective godly duties to each other, and an argument ensued. The wife said that she was "sick and tired of being told to submit to an undeserving husband." The husband said he could not imagine himself giving love and honor to a "wife who despised me." The problem with that couple, as is with many others, is that they misunderstood the Lord's commandments and ways and relied on the carnal law of quid pro quo (I will not give in unless there is something there for me). Obedience to God's commandments must be implicit—without reservations and preconditions—and regardless to what another does. It is a matter between us as individuals and God. We should never let another's behavior force us to offend God.

Now it may seem very hard, if not impossible, to comply with all of God's rules, or burden, as many refer to the commandments of God. So many people in the Christendom have resolved in their hearts and also have taught others that God's standards are burdensome, grievous, and beyond the ability of humans to comply with. This is rather very unfortunate, and the explanation below will reveal the untruth. The devil has done a tremendous job of successfully attacking our most important communion with God—implicit obedience as a manifestation of our love of God. There is absolutely no relationship with God devoid of obedience. Therefore, by casting fear on obedience to God, the enemy succeeds in his incessant effort to separate us from our Father. The most valuable thing to God is His word, and the devil's greatest fear is our obedience of the word of God, not the recitation of it.

Let us all take a deep breath and invite the Holy Spirit to quicken our understanding of the "burden" of God as we pause here to examine the burden and yoke of God.

THE BURDEN AND YOKE OF GOD

God, who cannot lie or deceive, has, since the beginning, pleaded with His children to seek the easy and light way to life—His way. Yet we humans have consistently rebelled against God's ways, saying that the ways of the Lord are heavy and burdensome.

The thoughts of God are continually of good for those who love Him. He has also promised not to demand of us more than we can handle, being privy to our frame. It is for our own good that the Lord asked us to take His burden and yoke. For while we can only think and guess, God alone knows what is best for us. Hence, many people hardly accept the loving invitation: "Come to Me, all you who labor and are heavy laden, and I will give you rest. Take my yoke upon you and learn from Me, for I am gentle and lowly in heart, and you will find rest for your souls, For My yoke is easy and My burden is light" (Mt 11:28-30). There is only one way to the divine rest for our souls—accepting the yoke and burden of God. The yoke and burden of this world is vanity and death, for they are all perishable; and in the end, we find out, as King Solomon did, that we have labored in vain. For in truth, we must leave all behind when the end comes. As the Preacher appropriately said, "'Vanity of Vanities,' says the Preacher. 'Vanity of vanities, all is vanity'" (Eccl 1:2). There is only one thing that is imperishable and needful for us—divine rest in the kingdom of God. The sooner we truly comprehend and live this obvious truth, the better for us. We should therefore do whatever it takes, including, if necessary, losing our physical lives for that which is eternal.

Chapter Fourteen

THE MYSTERY OF THE BURDEN OF JOSHUA

The mystery of the burden of Joshua is also God's divine formula to overcome all overwhelming situations and to obtain all the blessings, healing, prosperity, and all the good things we can and cannot imagine. Our case study will review the book of Joshua 1:5-9.

We read that after the death of Moses, God commanded Joshua, Moses's servant, to proceed to the promised land at the face of overwhelming obstacles and opposition (giants) while assuring him, thus: "No man shall be able to stand before you all the days of your life" (Jo 1:5). Then, God told Joshua that he (Joshua) needed three things: be strong and be of good courage and fear not (see Jo 1:6). Now, what did God command Joshua to be strong and of good courage about? Your answer may be as incorrect as mine and many others who have had this question put before them, for I assume you may say because of the overwhelming challenges and battles (giants) ahead of Joshua. But that is far from the correct reason. Joshua's only burden or challenge was for him to be strong and very courageous and

The Mystery Of The Burden Of Joshua

fearless in observing the commandments of the Lord, his God. God was admonishing Joshua never to turn to the left or to the right, never to compromise or be distracted in observing to do all His commandments. "Only be strong and very courageous, that you may observe to do according to all the law, which Moses My servant commanded you: do not turn from it to the right hand or to the left, that you may prosper wherever you go" (Jo 1:7). In other words, God told Joshua that all he needed to do was to implicitly obey Him (never compromise by any means), and if he did that, he would prosper wherever he went. Why? Because through implicit obedience, he would become one with God; and since the battle is the Lord's, not Joshua's, his way would be prosperous, and no one (man, demon, witchcraft, weapon, etc.) would be able to stand against him because the Lord would be his shepherd.

As if to leave nothing in doubt to Joshua, and all of us who are of Him, the Lord plainly stated to Joshua, thus, "This Book of the Law shall not depart from your mouth, but you shall meditate in it day and night, that you may observe to do according to all that is written in it. For then you will make your way prosperous, and then you will have good success" (Jo 1:8). In other words, if Joshua would eat, breathe, and live the commandments of his God without compromise, then and only then would he make his way prosperous and successful because God would dwell in him, fighting the battle for him. And who could stand against Joshua if God was with him?

Sadly, most people run all over the globe seeking for God's miracles, healing, prosperity, signs, wonders, deliverance and liberation, and all the deceptively coined names, not understanding the mystery surrounding the burden of Joshua. If we will understand that if the kingdom of God is within us, our needs and all things created by God are subject to us only if we gladly accept the light and easy yoke and burden of our God. We make our way prosperous and successful through implicit obedience to all of God's commandments. For then, if we do that, we will not have to worry about the battle or any weapons formed against us or any situation whatsoever. For the Lord will be with us; and if the Lord is with us, who can be against us? Putting it another way, God literally said to Joshua, Do what I command you, and I will do my part, which you can't do. Therefore, it is prudent for us to worry about only those things we can do—seek first the kingdom and God's righteousness. It is no wonder then why the Lord referred to His yoke as light and easy.

The apostle John also said that the commandments (burdens) of God are not burdensome. "For this is the love of God, that we keep His commandments. And His commandments are not burdensome" (1 Jn 5:3). And how true is it? To answer this question, we must comprehend and appreciate what God requires of us. "And now, Israel, what does the Lord your God require of you, but to fear the Lord your God, to walk in all His ways and to love Him, to serve the Lord your God with all your heart and all your soul, and to keep the commandments of the Lord and His statutes which I command you today for your good?" (Dt 10:12-13). Now, let us pause here to personalize this scripture for the moment. The only reason God wants us to obey Him is so that it will be well with us (for our own good). Besides, the Lord does not require us to have physical fear of Him but rather that we should depart from evil (see Prv 8:13). If anyone desires a simple and peaceful life to eternity, let him live the word implicitly (see Ps 15, 34:12-14). Again, King Solomon, in the exercise of the divine wisdom given to him by God and after he had seen and tasted all the things of the world concluded that the whole duty of man is to fear God (depart from evil) and obey Him. "Let us hear the conclusion of the whole matter: Fear God and keep His commandments, for this is the whole duty of man" (Eccl 12:13). Even we humans strive, in all sincerity and God-given ability, to imbibe in our children to shun evil and embrace good. Departing from evil is a demonstration of our love and fear of God, and the only way to effectuate that love is through implicit obedience. So the conclusion of life, or rather the purpose (beginning and ending of life), is to fear God and obey Him. Therefore, the whole or only duty of humans is anchored on love and obedience—the two keys to the kingdom of God. Without which, no one shall see the Lord. Hence, the Lord said, "But seek first the kingdom of God, and His righteousness, and all these things shall be added to you" (Mt 6:33). Again, our love and obedience must be perfect as God is perfect, for those born of God are created after God in righteousness and holiness (see Mt 5:48; Eph 4:24). If we Christians can understand and appreciate this mystery, we shall know that the burden of God is the greatest simplifier of life. It is a blessing indeed when we understand that there is one—and only one—Master to please.

Chapter Fifteen

THE GREATEST SPIRITUAL VICTORY

Let me, from the onset, dispel a misconception among many of us. The greatest spiritual victory is certainly not praying or fasting or worshipping or prophesying or speaking in tongues or preaching the Gospel, but is rather to get to the heart of God by way of perfect love and doing all things to God's glory and not to man. This is being led by the Sprit of God in righteousness and holiness. Therefore, the way to righteousness and holiness is to do whatever we do to God alone. If we do all things to God, we shall see Him and even prosper on this earth. Whatever that is done in fear of or to be seen by or admired or hailed by or to please a human being borders on selfishness, self-preservation, self-exaltation, eye service, and pride—all of which are abominations to God. Blessed is the one who seeks not his own glory or for others to glorify him. Even more, blessed is the one who, from the heart, shares not God's glory. God is the only one to please, and when we please Him, we have pleased all, except the devil; and we are not to please the devil. The only formula to simplify our life is to strive, at all cost, to please God, for God is all about goodness, righteousness, justice, fairness, and above all, perfect love. "And whatever you do in word or deed, do all in the name of the Lord Jesus, giving thanks to God the Father through Him. And whatever you do, do it heartily, as to the Lord and not to men" (Col 3:17, 23). A born of God desires his reward only from the Lord and not from man. Therefore, in whatever situation we find ourselves (jobs, church settings, leadership or servant roles, etc.), we should strive to please God no matter the consequences. Again, as the apostle Paul said, "Bondservants, be obedient to those who are your masters according to the flesh, with fear and trembling, in sincerity of heart, as to Christ; not with eye service, as men-pleasers, but as bondservants of Christ, doing the will of God from the heart, with goodwill doing service, as to the Lord, and not to men" (Eph 6:5-7). The apostle Paul drove this point home again in his First Epistle to the Corinthians as follows: "Therefore, whether you eat or drink, or whatever you do, do all to the glory of God" (1 Cor 10:31). Whatever we do that does not glorify God glorifies the devil and things of the devil.

CONSEQUENCES OF NOT DOING ALL THINGS FOR GOD

For a true child of God, whatever we do, whether good or bad, must be done for God alone. To truly understand and live this biblical truth is the greatest spiritual victory. We will examine just four examples of those who feared people rather than God.

   a. *King Saul.* For fear of his men and to please them, King Saul failed to implicitly obey God. Rather, he had a partial obedience to the mandate of God; and when the prophet Samuel confronted him, he (Saul) became belligerent and exhibited a stubborn, unrepentant heart. But when he realized the wrath of God against him, he confessed that his disobedience was a result of fear of people. Hear King Saul, "I have sinned, for I have transgressed the commandment of the Lord and your words, because I feared the people, and obeyed their voice" (1 Sm 15:24). And the prophet Samuel said to King Saul, "Has the Lord as great delight in burnt offerings and sacrifices, as in obeying the voice of the Lord? Behold, to obey is better than sacrifice, and to heed than the fat of rams" (1 Sm 15:22). As a consequence of his disobedience, God rejected him forever; and worst still, the people he feared couldn't save him.

b. *King David and Bathsheba.* King David, as we read, committed adultery with Bathsheba, and in an effort to cover his sin and the pregnancy as a result of it, he proceeded to devise ways to eliminate Uriah the Hittite, Bathsheba's husband. David, as king, felt he had scored a home run and that his secret was buried with Uriah. But he forgot that nothing could be hidden from the omnipotent and omnipresent God, whether He (God) chooses to expose or cover it. To King David's detriment, and as an example for us, God sent the prophet Nathan to confront David and pronounce His punishment for the crime (see 2 Sm 12:1-11). Incidentally, there are so many people who think it well that they have smartly covered their sins just simply because God has graciously not allowed them to be exposed. Such people are consumed by their fear of other people and what they will think of them. But they forget to their detriment that the only one to fear is God, and the only way to fear God is to depart from evil and the appearance of evil.

c. *Ananias and Sapphira.* In an apparent effort to impress the apostles and be admired of others, Ananias and his wife, Sapphira, conspired to conceal the actual sale price of their land by keeping back part of the money and lying about it. In response to their deception, the apostle Peter made a chilling reprimand, which, to this day, most of us pay a lip service to; for while we enjoy reading and citing that scripture, we conveniently refuse to take it seriously to heart and tremble at the reading of it. But Peter said, "Ananias, why has Satan filled your heart to lie to the Holy Spirit and keep back part of the price of the land for yourself? You have not lied to men but to God" (Acts 5:3-4). Whatever a child of God does, he does it to God, whether good or evil. Each time we lie, for example, we lie against God, who searches and knows the hearts and thoughts of people. We know the fate of Ananias and his wife, which God set as a vivid warning for all.

d. *The apostle Peter.* Another striking example of not doing things for God was the hypocritical reaction exhibited by apostle Peter for fear of people. In the past, Peter had fellowship freely with the Gentiles, but in the presence of the Jews, who were uncompromising in the tradition of circumcision, he would have nothing to do with Gentiles, thereby living a double and false life. "Now When Peter had come to Antioch, I withstood him to his face because he was to be blamed; For before certain men came from

James, he would eat with the Gentiles; but when they came, he withdrew and separated himself, fearing those who were of the circumcision" (Gal 2:11-12).

The common factor among the four examples above is that the subjects desired to please people rather than God. Their main concern was people—to please and cover their transgressions from them. They sought to look good outwardly rather than be good. For this reason, the Lord admonished us, thus: "And do not fear those who kill the body but cannot kill the soul. But rather fear Him who is able to destroy both soul and body in hell" (Mt 10:28). "I, even I, am He who comforts you. Who are you that you should be afraid of a man who will die, and of the son of a man who will be made like grass, and you forget the Lord your maker" (Is 51:12-13).

It is a catastrophic misplacement of priority when the reason we live and restrain ourselves is our fear of people. This is rather a curse, for it's written: Thus says the Lord, "Cursed is the man who trusts in man and makes flesh his strength, whose heart departs from the Lord" (Jer 17: 5). And why should we not put our trust in anyone other than God? Because, "The heart is deceitful above all things, and desperately wicked; who can know it?" (Jer 17: 9). The mystery surrounding this is not in the obvious fact that the heart is deceitful, but rather "who can know it." Since only God knows the heart, He alone deserves to be revered and trusted. For in truth, we fear those we strive to please. I have always cited this hypothetical example wherever this topic was taught, and most people can relate to it. I have a wife, and whenever we are together, boy, I shower her with so much love and emotion. But no sooner I am out of her presence, especially if I travel far from her, lo and behold, a *macho* tiger is born.

Without any restraint, I will assume another role to other women. You see, the one I fear in that instance is my wife; hence, I try very hard to please her by hiding the dark side of me from her. But can anyone hide from the omnipresent God? While I must love, honor, and respect my wife, God alone, who sees in secret, deserves my fear and obedience. For we can run, but we can't hide from Him.

Imagine all the crafty and complicated devices employed by us to hide evil from the eyes of others rather than strive to please God. This African folk story appropriately illustrates this issue. A man went to steal some property and asked his son to accompany him as a lookout. The man asked his son to watch for any movement in front, at the back, and to the right and left. And the son answered, "Father who is to watch the movement from above?" As it is written, "'Can anyone hide himself in secret places, so I shall not see him?' says the Lord. 'Do I not fill heaven and earth?'" (Jer 23:24). "Woe to those who seek deep to hide their counsel far from the Lord, and their works are in the dark; they say, 'Who sees us?' 'And who knows us?'" (Is 29:15). And as the Lord said, "For there is nothing hidden which will not be revealed, nor has anything been kept secret but that it should come to light" (Mk 4:22). It is a blessing when our sins are covered by God. "Blessed is he whose transgression is forgiven, whose sin is covered. Blessed is the man to whom the Lord does not impute iniquity" (Ps 32:1-2).

Even in most churches, the pastors seek to please the members, preaching and teaching Psychology 101's feel-good doctrine, telling the members what they (members) want to hear—the so-called positive and sweet messages—so as to win their approval and pockets while compromising the truth of the Gospel of Jesus Christ. This is not doing things unto God; rather, it is a tragedy, which God abhors. For whomever we do things to is the one we believe in, and the one we believe in is the one we serve and glorify, and the one we glorify is our god. We know our God is the only God—a jealous God who does not share His glory with anyone. For if we seek man's reward, the reward of God is exceedingly greater. As it is written, "Eye has not seen, nor ear heard, nor have entered into the heart of man the things which God has prepared for those who love Him" (1 Cor 2:9). Whoever pleases people rather than God is not of God. As apostle Paul rightly wrote to the church of God of Galatia, "For do I now persuade men, or God? Or do I seek to please men? For if I still please men, I would not be a bondservant of Christ" (Gal 1:10).

BLESSINGS FROM DOING THINGS FOR GOD

Let us now examine four examples of those who, in the most stressful circumstances, remained immovable rocks, uncompromising—with complete disregard to the possible consequences, opposition, pressure, and self-preservation—and against all odds, did things to God:

    a. *Joseph.* One glaring example of a person who did things to God rather than compromise for the pleasure of the moment was Joseph, the son of Jacob. Joseph, as we recall, had two similar dreams of the same interpretation. He dreamed that he was so elevated that his siblings and parents bowed before him. Fueled by long-standing envy because he was his father's favorite, his siblings resented him the more when he told them of his dreams; and when opportunity presented itself, they sold him into slavery. But God was with Joseph and prospered the works of his hands, such that his master made him the overseer of his (master's) affairs. Perhaps Joseph felt very good because the master respected and entrusted everything to him. What Joseph did not realize, however, was that while he was enrolled in the school of God (school of brokenness, humility, submission, surrender, refinement, and transformation), only God knew when he would graduate. The joy of his accomplishment was cut short by another test, occasioned by the pressure of his master's wife to get him to commit adultery. Most men, I suppose, would have gladly took her for it; after all, it would be relishing for them to share with the master his most treasured possession, and besides, the pleasure of the moment would be highly appealing. Not only that, no one except the two would have been privy to the deed, and the secret might remain forever with them. To most people, even the thought and desire to have it all and now would have been most compelling. But Joseph realized that there was only one needful and imperishable thing and that committing adultery would be sinning against God alone, hence this most impactful statement: "How then can I do this great wickedness, and sin against God?" (Gn 39:9). Joseph feared the only one who could see in secret and able to kill and cast people to hell. Joseph was not concerned about displeasing the human master, who might never find out; rather, he feared the one greater than the master and his house—the omnipresent God. Well, as the story went, Joseph suffered for his righteousness but kept his soul and integrity; and in the end, he had the last laugh. Referring to the faithful endurance of Moses, the scripture says, "By faith Moses, when he became of age, refused to be called the son of Pharaoh's daughter, choosing rather to suffer affliction with the people of God than to enjoy the passing pleasures of sin" (Heb 11:24-25). Again, the apostle Peter comforted us, thus: "Therefore let those who suffer according to the will of God commit their souls to Him in doing good, as to a faithful Creator" (1 Pt 4:19). Knowing of a certainty, if we remain steadfast and endure with thanksgiving, eventually, "all things work together for good to those who love God" (Rom 8:28).

b. *David and Saul and David at Ziklag*. Although David sinned against God in more ways than one, he demonstrated why he was a man after God's heart. In more than one occasion, God delivered King Saul into David's hands. Rather than take the matter into his hands, or bow to the pressure of his followers to kill King Saul, the fear of God restrained him. David was even convicted for cutting off his enemy's shirts. Hear him as he said to his men, "The Lord forbid that I should do this thing unto my master, the Lord's anointed, to stretch out my hand against him, seeing he is the anointed of the Lord" (1 Sm 24:6). The second time around, David commanded his captain of host to spare Saul's life. And David said to Abishai, "Do not destroy him; for who can stretch out his hand against the Lord's anointed, and be guiltiness?" (1 Sm 26:9).

The Greatest Spiritual Victory

The other instance was at his camp in Ziklag. David and his followers returned to their camp only to discover that all they had (wives, children, and property) had been carried away by the Amalekites. David was subjected to the most stressful test; even his followers spoke of stoning him. Nevertheless, rather than succumb to human pressure, he submitted himself to God, inquiring from, and encouraging himself in the Lord. "Now David was greatly distressed, for the people spoke of stoning him, because the soul of all the people was grieved, every man for his sons and for his daughters But David strengthened himself in the Lord his God" (1 Sm 30:6). So David inquired of the Lord, saying, "Shall I pursue this troop? Shall I overtake them?" And He answered him, "Pursue, for you shall surely overtake them and without fail recover all" (1 Sm 30:8). In other words, David was not going to offend God even if it meant the loss of everything, including his life. Rather, he chose to please the Giver rather than the gift.

c. *Job.* The story of Job is an epitome of enduring affliction and doing all things for God, even at the most breaking point. The first test came when Job's wife pleaded for him to curse God and die. But Job hushed her, and his words remind us that we should be prepared to receive good and evil with thanksgiving. "Shall we indeed accept good from God, and shall we not accept adversity? In all this Job did not sin with his lips" (Jb 2:10). Even when affliction, pain, and pressure became humanly unbearable, Job gave us this startling encouragement: "Though He slay me, yet will I trust Him. Even so I will defend my own ways before Him" (Jb 13:15).

d. *Shadrach, Meshach, and Abednego.* These were the three Jewish men who exhibited absolute faith and trust in the Lord. At the risk of being incinerated in the furnace of fire, these three men maintained themselves in the Lord and did all things to God rather than fear King Nebuchadnezzar and bow to an idol. Their response at the breaking point is the most powerful. "If that is the case, our God whom we serve is able to deliver us from the burning fiery furnace, and He will deliver us from your hand, O king. But if not, let it be known to you, O king, that we do not serve your gods, nor will we worship the gold image which you have set up" (Dn 3:17-18). In other words, these uncompromising men believed and trusted that God would deliver them from mortal danger, and even if He chose not to deliver them from the fiery furnace, He was still their God. That is it, for good or for bad, He is God, and whatever He decides is right and just. What a demonstration of absolute faith.

Chapter Sixteen

THE MYSTERY OF JUDAH, THE SON OF JACOB

DOING THINGS FOR GOD—
THE GREATEST SPIRITUAL VICTORY

During the days of my evangelistic work in Africa, the Lord woke me up very early one morning and said to me, "I will reveal to you the mysteries of the kingdom of God surrounding doing all things to God alone." He then pointedly asked me, "Of the twelve sons of Jacob, who received the covenant of Abraham, who was more blessed and favored among all of them?" Of course, I confidently and assuredly answered, "Joseph." This is the same answer I got from every congregation I have had the opportunity to share this topic. Perhaps Joseph is your answer. After all, Joseph was the beloved of his father, Jacob, and the one who was chosen to save Israel from famine. However, the Lord told me that I was wrong, and that *Judah*, not Joseph, was the covenant child of Israel. Then the Lord took me through a mystery journey of the single reason why Judah was more favored and blessed than all his brothers. Let us be mindful from the onset that Judah was neither the first nor the second nor the third, but rather, the fourth son of Jacob. So how then did the fourth son jump all the way to be the first? That is the mystery. At least we know that there was nothing spectacular or out of the ordinary at Judah's birth. We also know that Joseph was the favored son of the father and the envy of his siblings; it was Joseph who was given the dreams of greatness, so much so that his parents and brothers would bow before him, which dreams were fulfilled thirteen years later in Egypt. Notwithstanding, God established His covenant with Judah. I invite you now to take this mystery journey of the kingdom of God with me.

The Lord asked me to read the book of Psalms 78:67-71: "Moreover He rejected the tent of Joseph, and did not choose the tribe of Ephraim. But chose the tribe of Judah, Mount Zion which He loved. And He built His sanctuary like the heights, like the earth which He has established forever."

"Wow!" I said after reading the above-referenced scriptures. Although I had read the Bible, I never seemed, at any time, to take note or understand the seriousness of the cited passages. The Lord made it clear that He rejected Joseph and others but chose and established Judah forever. We will recall that the Lord promised an everlasting kingdom to David, a descendant of Judah. Then, the Lion of the Tribe of Judah, the Lord, Jesus Christ, proceeded from the tribe of Judah, and His rule shall never end.

Again, the Lord asked me to read the Gospel of Matthew 1:2: "Abraham begot Isaac, Isaac begot Jacob, and Jacob begot Judah and his brothers." Then, the Lord asked if I understood, and I answered, "No, Lord." Then, He said, "Imagine a man

The Mystery Of Judah, The Son Of Jacob

who has twelve sons and the name of one of them is John. As part of his genealogical history, he is only known or referred to as the father of John and others as if the others do not matter, yet John is not his first son, but the fourth." I then understood the serious implication of this scripture passage. A reading of the Gospel of Matthew 1:3 reveals the genealogical linage of Abraham continued from Judah to Phares, Judah's son with Tamar. The Lord asked if I understood then, and I answered yes. But I was still lost as to the reason Judah was favored. Again, the Lord asked me to read the book of Judges 1:1-2 "Now after the death of Joshua, it came to pass, that the children of Israel asked the Lord, saying, 'Who shall be first to go up for us against the Canaanites, to fight against them?' And the Lord said, 'Judah shall go up. Indeed I have delivered the land into his hand.'" Then the Lord asked if I understood that, and I said, "Yes, Lord." Now come to think of it, after the death of Joshua, when the children of Israel inquired of the Lord concerning the promised land, He literally told them that He had given the land to Judah. But why Judah was so favored remained a mystery to me.

Again, the Lord asked me to read the book of Genesis 49:8-10: "Judah, you are he whom your brothers shall praise; your hand shall be on the neck of your enemies; your father's children shall bow down before you. The scepter shall not depart from Judah, nor a lawgiver from between his feet, until Shiloh comes; and to him shall be the obedience of the people" (Gn 49:8, 10).

"Wow!" I said again. I thought it was Joseph whom the brethren should bow to according to his dreams, which were fulfilled in Egypt. Then it became obviously clear to me that although Joseph was chosen to save Israel from starvation, the true everlasting covenant child was Judah. And as long as the earth remains, the staff of leadership/kingship (scepter) shall never depart from the tribe of Judah. Yet the reason why Judah was the chosen one out of the twelve sons of Jacob remained a mystery. To unveil this mystery, the Lord asked me to read the book of Genesis 29:30-35.

As a prelude to understanding these scriptural verses, the following facts emerge: Jacob (Israel) had two wives, namely, Leah and Rachel. While Leah was not so loved by Jacob, Rachel, on the other hand, was his beloved. The just God had pity on Leah and blessed her with children while Rachel suffered the agony of barrenness for a while. "When the Lord saw that Leah was unloved, He opened her womb; but Rachel was barren" (Gn 29:31). The dramatic events leading to the mystery unfolded as Leah conceived and bore her sons. "So Leah conceived and bore a son, and she called his name Reuben; for she said, 'The Lord has surely looked on my affliction, now therefore, my husband will love me'" (Gn 29:32). The Lord asked me, "What was important to Leah following the birth of her first son?" I replied that Leah's main concern was the love and affection of her husband. Again, the Lord asked me to read the next verse: "Then she conceived again and bore a son, and said, 'Because the Lord has heard that I am unloved, He has therefore given me this son also': and she called his name Simeon" (Gn 29:33).

Again, the Lord asked me what was important to Leah at the birth of her second son. And I gave the same answer—her husband's love. And again, the Lord asked me to read on: "She conceived again and bore a son, and said, 'Now this time my husband will become attached to me, because I have borne him three sons.' Therefore was his name called Levi" (Gn 29:34).

And once again, the Lord asked me to read the next verse: "And she conceived again and bore a son, and she said, 'Now will I praise the Lord.' Therefore she called his name Judah. Then she stopped bearing" (Gn 29:35). And the Lord said to me, "You see, I chose Judah and blessed him above all his brothers because at his birth, Leah gave Me alone the glory". Then the Lord referred me to the book of Isaiah 42:8: "I am the Lord, that is My name; and My glory will I not give to another, nor My praise to carved images."

The above revelation of the hidden mystery of the kingdom of God says it all about doing all things for God and not to man. When we, from our hearts, do all things for God, He alone receives the exclusive glory; and His blessings are poured out abundantly on us. Doing all things for God is an obvious demonstration of spiritual hunger for Him and that He alone matters above every human being or thing. This is the ultimate, greatest spiritual victory.

Looking back at the mystery, we quickly find that not until the birth of Judah did Leah truly pour out her heart to the only one who had given her both the children and her husband. The more God blessed her, the more consumed she was with her desire to win the love of her husband until when Judah was born. Even when she had her third son, her only desire was that the husband would then "wrap" himself around her because she had given him a third son. As a matter of record, Leah desired the love and attention of her husband above all other things, including God, the Giver. As such, Leah lived only for Jacob and to please him alone. In other words, Leah worshipped the gift rather than the Giver. This is the case for many of us who have misplaced our priority—to please human beings for the pleasure and reward of the moment. Rather, we

The Two Keys To The Kingdom Of God

should seek to fear God and please Him alone (depart from evil and obey Him), no matter the opposition.

It is equally noteworthy to observe another folly in the saga of Leah. Subsequent to the birth of Judah, she used the occasions of the births of her other children to taunt and wage war of envy and words with her sister, Rachel. As far as God was concerned, Leah only got it right when Judah was born.

Doing all things to God by way of implicit obedience, out of sincere love, and reverence for His name brings everlasting blessings and generational inheritance (see Dt 5:29). Our God is so merciful and faithful; nevertheless, He is a jealous God who will never share His glory with anyone.

THE OTHER LESSON

There is one sad lesson that we must all learn from the relationship between the two sisters, Leah and Rachel. Rather than give God the glory that was rightly due to Him, the two sisters, like many of us, used the occasions of God's blessings to offend Him. As God blessed them with children, they employed the occasions to taunt and mock their enemies—themselves. In many cultures as it was in Israel, every name given to a child has a specific and deep-rooted emotional meaning. Oftentimes, even we Christians try to settle stupid scores and envy by giving names to our children, which reflect resentment toward our foes, thereby, unwittingly, giving the glory that is rightly God's to the devil. As we read further in the book of Genesis, chapter 30, we find that Leah was not only consumed by her desire for the husband, but no sooner she overcame that when she turned her attention to the little war of envy, jealousy, and resentment with her sister. The level of resentment so blinded her that at the birth of all her other children after Judah, she used the occasions to glorify the devil. As for Rachel, the beloved wife of Jacob, she was as much involved in the bitter war. When Bilhah (Rachel's maid) had a second son, rather than glorify God, Rachel said, "With great wrestlings I have wrestled with my sister, and indeed I have prevailed. So she called his name Naphtali" (Gn 30:8). When Leah saw this, she became more resentful and gave her maid to Jacob. And when her maid bore a son to Jacob, Leah said, "A troop comes! So she called his name Gad" (Gn 30:11). All along, in all these instances, God did not receive any glory because the glory was given to the devil. That is, of course, not doing things for God. So as we can observe, of all the twelve sons of Jacob, God and God alone received all the glory at the birth of Judah only.

And to Him, the only living God be all the glory now and forever. Amen.

Chapter Seventeen

THE BLESSINGS OF THE TWO KEYS

At the risk of surprising myself, let me now sing a song of blessings, prosperity, riches, wealth, miracles, etc., appertaining to the two keys to the kingdom of God. During the period of my in-house confinement, the Lord cautioned me, thus: "Never teach or preach prosperity, miracles, and healings, for these are the things I freely give to My children who love and obey Me, but when you pray for these things, I will grant your prayers." God is all about perfect love and implicit obedience; and whoever abides in these two keys is born of God, and the one who is born of God is one with Him in spiritual agreement and therefore a joint heir of the kingdom of God with our Lord, Jesus Christ.

This is the fusing-together relationship that makes all things of God ours. And since all things are created by Him and for His pleasure, it holds true, therefore, that all things seen and not seen are the inheritance of those who are born of God. Even the devil is subject to those who are of God through the two keys to the kingdom of God.

Therefore, the blessings of abiding in the two keys to the kingdom of God can simply be stated in one word: *everything*. The only way to unlock the door (Jesus) of the kingdom of God is through the use of the two keys, which are the subjects of this book. Whoever unlocks the door of the kingdom has eternal life, which incidentally is the only needful thing in life. Therefore, all things in heaven and on earth are ours if we are one with God. As the Lord said, "All things that the Father has are mine" (Jn 16:15). And this is as a result of oneness with the Father. "That they all may be one, as You, Father, are in Me, and I in You; that they also may be one in Us" (Jn 17:21). Therefore, to be one with God is a condition precedent to receiving all our needs according to His riches and perfect will. As has been stated in a previous chapter, our God is the God of "if." If we do what He requires and commands us to do, He will do His own part even more abundantly than we ask. Since this relationship with God is anchored on the two keys to His kingdom—love and obedience—it must, of necessity, hold true that these two keys are the keys to life, health, miracles, prosperity, healings, blessings, etc. Perfect love and obedience to the commandments of God make all things subject to those who are of God. "Therefore do not worry, saying, what shall we eat? Or what shall we drink? Or what shall we wear? For, after, all these things are what the Gentiles seek. For your heavenly Father knows that you need all these things. But seek first the kingdom of God and His righteousness, and all these things shall be added to you" (Mt 6:31-33). This scripture, like other similar ones, from the books of Genesis to Revelation respectively captures the character of God and is spiritually sufficient for this chapter. But how many times have we read and cited this scripture without truly committing it to heart? Sadly, as stated in a previous chapter, we are a generation of immediate gratification. We want it now, and we mean now; click here and it is done, lest we be offended. One thing is certain: we can change just about everything and at any time for our selfish purpose, but we can neither weary nor change God. God cannot and will never change for any one person or nation. He remains the same now and forever. He has laid a prescribed rule and way, and as long as He lives, His word abides forever. So the sooner we thankfully fall in line with His rule, the better for us. While it is perfectly all right to claim all the goodness of God and even for some ministers to encourage people with these promises once in a while, to make them the focus of feel-good teaching and preaching or to refuse to sincerely tell the members that where there is a blessing, there is also a curse associated with it and that we cannot get from point A to point B until we get to point A first is disingenuous at best and, at worst, abominable. The things of God involve a conscious choice. Moses was blunt about it with the congregation of the children of Israel. "Behold, I set before you today a blessing and a curse: the blessing if you obey the commandments of the Lord your God which I command you today, and the curse, if you do not obey the commandments" (Dt 11:26-28). And as we have read, God told Joshua that the only burden he had in order to make his way prosperous and successful was to be strong and to have a good courage in keeping God's commandments. One of the most cited scriptures reads as follows: "If My people who are called by My name will humble themselves, and pray and seek my face, and turn from their wicked ways, then I will hear from heaven, and will forgive their sins and heal their land" (2 Chr 7:14).

Very unfortunately, the truth is now discarded as judgmental or negative. This is a very sad trend in majority of churches worldwide. We shall be judged by the truth; therefore, we must return to the love of the truth or perish for rejecting the truth. A common African adage states that "what make good and tasty soup are the ingredients used to make it." Where there is no pain, there is no gain.

The book of Isaiah beautifully presents to us a divine invitation by our gracious Father to come and reason together with Him. "Wash yourself, make yourself clean; put away the evil of your doings from before My eyes. Cease to do evil, learn to do good; seek justice, rebuke the oppressor; Defend the fatherless, plead for the widow" (1:16-17). If we will do the above, the Lord invites us, "'Come now, and let us reason together,' says the Lord. 'Though your sins are like scarlet, they shall be as white as snow'" (Is 1:18). What an unbelievable divine gesture to reason together with our Father and our God. But there is a caveat (an *if*) to it: "If you are willing and obedient, you shall eat the good of the Land; But if you refuse and rebel, you shall be devoured by the sword" (Is 1:19-20).

I cannot simply recall the numerous times I have been confronted with arguments, which cite the scriptures in part only. One told me, "The word of God said that if I ask, I shall receive, seek I shall find, and knock it shall be opened to me." I reminded her that the scripture correctly says in full that if we abide in Jesus and His word abides in us, then whatever we ask in His name, we shall receive (see Jn 15:17). Needless to say, she had an issue (as she put it) with the "abiding part." But how can we receive from God if we are against Him? As it is written, "And whatever we ask we receive from Him, because we keep His commandments and do those things that are pleasing in His sight" (1 Jn 3:22). Another scripture that is widely cited in part is, "Resist the devil and he will flee from you" (Jas 4:7). We forget that if we do not submit to God first, the devil will not flee; and even at worse, we will suffer the same fate as the sons of Sceva (see Acts 19:13-16). It is in vain to ask contrary to the will of God, and that is what we do when we do not seek first His kingdom and His righteousness. As it is written, "Now this is the confidence we have in Him, that if we ask anything according to His will, He hears us" (1 Jn 5:14).

God is, and has always been, in the business of blessing and providing for His own, and total submission and dependence on Him by way of strict adherence to the prescribed rules of the two keys to His kingdom gets Him to lavishly pour His blessings on us beyond our expectations. Lack of the two keys leads us to misplace our priorities and inheritance for us and our children. "Oh, that there had such a heart in them that they would fear Me and always keep all My commandments, that it might be well with them and with their children for ever! (Dt 5:29).

Chapter Eighteen

WHAT ELSE?

The scripture admonishes us to examine every spirit that is teaching or preaching or speaking to us to know if it is of God. "Beloved, do not believe every spirit, but test the spirits, whether they are of God; because many false prophets have gone out into the world" (1 Jn 4:1). This scripture holds true today more than in the days of apostle John. There are many agents of darkness parading themselves all over the globe as ministers of Jesus Christ. He who is of God hears and loves the truth, which is the word of God, and the word of God remains true forever; the traditions, cultures, and desires of the world cannot alter it. Let me make this bold conclusion: Whoever deliberately preaches, teaches, practices, or encourages any doctrine contrary to the doctrine and word of Jesus Christ is an Antichrist. For whoever is not with Jesus is against Him (see Mt 12:30).

I pray that the Spirit of God will minister to your heart today. Today (now) is the acceptable time for a careful self-examination, with returning to the love of the truth as the only view; for in truth, the kingdom of God is nearer at hand than ever. When we take account of the numerous happenings around us, we are vividly reminded of our fragile nature. For no matter how hard we try, tomorrow remains unknown to us. The world, as we know it, shall pass away; but for those who are of God, the concern should not be the end of the world but the day of our individual end. This is the awesome greatness of God; human beings can think or guess, but only God knows, and in most cases, He tells no one.

Once again, as always, the Lord is using this medium to call on His rebellious children to return today to the first love—love of the truth. As it is written, "I have stretched out My hands all day long to a rebellious people, who walk in a way that is not good, according to their own thoughts" (Is 65:2). And He challenges us to witness against Him if He had, in any way, wronged us. Hear the Lord's plea, "O my people, what have I done to you? And how have I wearied you? Testify against Me" (Mi 6:3). For God came to us by way of His only begotten Son; He was sacrificed for our sake, yet we will not come to Him with all our heart. While agonizing over the sin committed by King David, the Lord wondered why David, whom He had given everything, would still transgress against Him. "I gave you your master's house and your master's wives into your keeping, and gave you the house of Israel and of Judah. And if that had been too little, I also would have given you much more! Why have you despised the commandment of the Lord, to do evil in His sight?" (2 Sm 12:8-9).

Even today, the Lord is asking us, "What else should I have done for you that I have not done already?" Now I urge you to take a moment and reflect on your God and Father mourning for His rebellious children, who have chosen the pleasure of the moment over the love of the truth. Hear, oh heavens, and give ear, oh earth, for the Lord has spoken: "I have nourished and brought up children, and they have rebelled against Me; The ox knows its owner and the donkey its master's crib; but Israel does know, My people do not consider" (Is 1:2-3). Yes, what else indeed should God do for us that he has not already done to give us life and truth? Even as He cried out the more at the destruction of His vineyard, "Now let Me sing to My well-beloved regarding His vineyard: My well-beloved has a vineyard on a very fruitful hill. He dug it up and cleared out its stones, and planted it with the choicest vine. He built a tower in its midst, and also made a winepress in it; So He expected it to bring forth good grapes, But it brought forth wild grapes. And now, O inhabitants of Jerusalem, and men of Judah, judge, please between Me and My vineyard. What more could have been done to my vineyard that I have not done in it? Why then, when I expected it to bring forth good grapes, Did it bring forth wild grapes?" (Is 5:1-4).

Now, take another moment and reflect on the agony of your God and Father, over His rebellious children who have turned away from the love of the truth. Even while hanging on the cross, being crucified for our sake, the Lord still reached out to us. "Father, forgive them, for they do not know what they do" (Lk 23:34). Now, what other excuse do we have for turning away from the love of the truth of God and going about to establish our own doctrine and standard of righteousness? The word of God is the truth and is God, and we are judged by the truth but cursed for rejecting the truth. If He had not come down from heaven to show the way of life and truth, we may be excused (see Jn 15:22). Or perhaps, the Lord shall plead for us as in the case of the parable of the barren fig tree: "Father, give them one more year, and if after that they remain unfruitful, they shall be cut down" (see Lk 13:6-9). But in truth, I say to all that our time is up, for the kingdom of God is nearer at hand than we think. As the apostle Paul firmly revealed in his opener of the Epistle to the Romans: "For the wrath of God is revealed from heaven against all ungodliness and unrighteousness of men, who suppress the truth in unrighteousness" (Rom 1:18). And how did they suppress the truth in unrighteousness? "Because what may be known of God is manifest in them, for God has shown it to them. For since the creation of the world His invisible attributes are clearly seen, being understood by the things that are made, even His eternal power and Godhead, so that they are without excuse, because, although they knew God, they did not glorify Him as God, nor were thankful, but became futile in their thoughts, and their foolish hearts were darkened" (Rom 1:19-21). As it is written: "God who at various times and in various ways spoke in time past to the fathers by the prophets, has in these last days spoken to us by His Son, whom He has appointed heir of all things, through whom He made the worlds; who being the brightness of His glory and the express image of His person, . . ." (Heb 1: 1-3). Simply put, God came down from heaven to show the truth and way to eternal life, but we prefer our own standard for our selfish ends. Nothing can be more true of the present state of churches of God worldwide than the above scripture passages. As apostle Paul rightly stated, he obtained mercy because he acted ignorantly (see 1 Tm 1:13). What does this tell us if we presumptuously turn away from the love of the truth? As is the case these days, where then comes mercy?

For this reason, the Lord is asking today, "Where are My elect when the love of the truth is being trampled on and craftily suppressed and manipulated? And where is My watchman, and why is he asleep as the thief comes to steal and destroy? And where is My intercessor to plead for My mercy? And where is My point of contact for he is disconnected from Me? Should not the sign point the way? should not the watchman safeguard? should not the intercessor plead for mercy? should not the point of contact be connected in agreement with the source? and should not the pastor preserve the vineyard rather than destroy and plunder it? The whole place is polluted, and My houses of worship are defiled and they stink; and I look down from heaven, and I see not My elect nor My sign nor My watchman nor My intercessor nor My point of contact, for all have gone astray after their own lusts and belly, and what with itching ears hungry to hear what they want to hear, things that make them feel good, and with false teachers and prophets to tell them sweet lies, as well as deceivers, liars, and manipulators who heap around them; they gather for their own pleasure and lusts, not surely altogether in My name. And with their hearts very far from Me, they commit abomination before My face, turning My houses of worship into houses of merchandise, manipulation, lies, and deceit."

As it is written, "Will you steal, murder, commit adultery, swear falsely, burn incense to Baal, and walk after other gods whom you do not know, and then come and stand before Me in this house which is called by My name, and say, 'we are delivered to do all these abominations'? "Has this house, which is called by My name, become a den of thieves in your eyes? Behold, I, even I, have seen it," says the Lord. (Jer 7:9-11).

"Return now to Me," says the Lord of Hosts. "Pull down and put away those altars of manipulation, deceit, and idolatry; do well, and eschew evil and appearance of evil; return to the love of the truth of My Gospel and doctrine; and I will receive you. Let those who manipulate, deceive, and lie in My name cease to do so today and repent of their sins. For cursed is he who deceives others in My name, and woe to him who is deceived. But cursed to the deceiver and the deceived when the deceived who has heard the truth and should have known the truth turns away from it and invites the deceiver." For it is written, "Bread gained by deceit is sweet to a man, but afterward his mouth will be filled with gravel" (Prv 20:17).

There is only one Lord, Jesus Christ, and only one God and one doctrine according to Jesus Christ. And whoever teaches or preaches or practices another doctrine contrary to the doctrine of Jesus Christ is against Him. As the apostle John wrote in his Second Epistle, "Whoever transgresses and does not abide in the doctrine of Christ does not have God. He that abides in the doctrine of Christ has both the Father and the Son" (1-9). The apostle Paul, writing to Timothy, warned us seriously, "If anyone teaches otherwise and does not consent to the wholesome words, even the words of our Lord Jesus Christ, and to the doctrine which accords with godliness, he is proud, knowing nothing, but is obsessed with disputes and arguments over words, from which come envy, strife, reviling, evil suspicions, useless wranglings of men of corrupt minds, and destitute of the truth, who suppose that godliness is a means of gain. From such withdraw yourself" (1 Tm 6:3-5). The apostle John also warned us not to associate or give room to such deceivers. "If anyone comes to you and does not bring this doctrine, do not receive him into your house nor greet him; For he who greets him shares in his evil deeds" (2 Jn 1:10-11).

I sincerely believe there has never been a more dangerous time than the present time we are in, what with the proliferation of churches and false teachers, preachers, and prophets running in the millions, being let loose in the world, deceiving and being deceived. And what with itching ears of many members, they make merchandise of them under the color of the authority of the Gospel of Jesus Christ, forsaking the love of the truth, and, with extraordinary gifts of oratory and auctioneer's enticing words, turn the souls of many away from life and truth—repentance, salvation, love, forgiveness, mercy, kindness, and implicit obedience.

The Bible is full of warnings of false teachers and preachers who parade themselves as angels of light while in reality, they work only for their bellies. There is no worse season than this time when many people have their conscience seared against the truth. "Now the Spirit expressly says that in the latter times some will depart from the faith, giving heed to deceiving spirits and doctrines of demons, speaking lies in hypocrisy, having their own conscience seared with a hot iron" (1 Tm 4:1-2). "But evil men and impostors will grow worse and worse, deceiving and being deceived" (2 Tm 3:13).

The Lord, Jesus Christ, and His apostles warned us of the danger and season when these manipulators, deceivers, and liars would be ushered in. But I tell you, that season is now when the quest is for meganumber, and the familiar spirit, prosperity and fame rather than the love of the truth. Therefore, it behooves the elect of God to watch and to be on guard for their souls. "For false Christ and false prophets will rise and show great signs and wonders to deceive, if possible, even the elect" (Mt 24:24). And who is he that is deceived? Those who have turned away from the uncompromising truth of the Gospel and doctrine of Jesus Christ. "The coming of the lawless one is according to the working of Satan, with all power, signs and lying wonders, and with all unrighteousness deception among those who perish, because they did not receive the love of the truth, that they might be saved" (2 Thes 2:9-10). As a consequence of rejection of the love of the truth, the wrath of God is poured on disobedient and rebellious people. "And for this reason God will send them strong delusion, that they should believe the lie, that they all may be condemned who did not believe the truth but had pleasure in unrighteousness" (2 Thes 2:11-12). Again and again, the Bible leaves us with no doubt of this season we are in, when the uncompromising preaching and teaching of the undiluted truth of the Gospel of Jesus Christ is considered and even labeled as unpopular, offensive, aggressive, old-fashioned, judgmental, condemnatory, strong, insensitive, condescending, negative, politically incorrect, and out of tone with the current way of life. Addressing this issue, the apostle Paul wrote to Timothy, thus: "Preach the word!, be ready in season and out of season. Convince, rebuke, exhort, with all long suffering and teaching. For the time will come when they will not endure sound doctrine, but according to their own desires, because they have itching ears, they will heap up for themselves teachers; and they will turn their ears away from the truth, and be turned aside to fables" (2 Tm 4:2-4). The apostle Paul lived this uncompromising truth of the Gospel of the kingdom, not minding what it caused him, but in the end, he maintained his integrity and received the crown of life. While facing all manners of persecution for the truth, he boldly declared, "Serving the Lord with all humility, with many tears and trials which happened to me by the plotting of the Jews; how I kept back nothing that was helpful, but proclaimed it to you, have taught you publicly" (Acts 20:19-20).

Despite all the evils against him, Paul never compromised or preached to please anyone. "But none of these things move me; nor do I count my life dear to myself, so that I may finish my race with joy, and the ministry which I received from the Lord Jesus" (Acts 20:24). Even more important to Paul was that he was not guilty of anyone's blood through deceit, manipulation, and lies. "Therefore I testify to you this that I am innocent of the blood of all men. For I have not shunned to declare to you the whole counsel of God" (Acts 20:26-27). So let all be warned! For no matter what we want or say or feel or do, God remains God of the Ancient of Ages, unchangeable, and His truth lives forever. While the truth may be bitter, nevertheless, it is life and spirit (see Jn 6:63). Therefore, beloved of the Lord, let us return today (now) to our God and to His truth. Let us seek Him while we still have breath in us, redeeming the time, for the kingdom of God is nearer at hand, and no one knows tomorrow.

I am not unmindful that some readers may consider this book sensitive and a no-go area while others may quickly conclude that some of its contents are judgmental and condemnatory as the truth of the Gospel is casually waved off these days. Neither the entire book nor any of its contents falls into such negative classification. The last thing this book is intended to accomplish is to judge or to condemn anyone, but rather it intends to get the children of God to return to Him and His righteousness. For how can I judge or condemn others when I cannot even judge me? As the Lord revealed to me, for one to judge and condemn others, he must either be perfect or has ownership rights or has been commissioned by the owner to do so. Since God is perfect and has ownership of all flesh, He alone justifies. And since God alone knows tomorrow, it is only prudent for us to walk in agreement with Him. But if we perceive the truth of God's word as judgmental, then the churches of God have lost the battle, and Christ has died and risen in vain. The Lord has given us not the spirit of timidity and compromise but of sound mind and boldness in the defense of the Gospel. For we must be judged and condemned by the word, for God and His word are the same. "'Is not My word like a fire?' says the Lord. 'And like a hammer that breaks the rock in pieces?'" (Jer 23:29). "For the word of God is living and powerful, and sharper than any two-edged sword, piercing even to the division of soul and spirit, and of joints and marrow, and is a discerner of the thoughts and intents of the heart. And there is no creature hidden from His sight, but all things are naked and open to the eyes of Him to whom we must give account" (Heb 4:12-13).

We should carefully reflect on this two-edged sword for a moment. It cuts either way, keeping alive those who use it properly and killing those who misuse and abuse it. And it shall never pass away because it is the truth and the most treasured thing of God. Incidentally, the most thing the devil fears is our implicit adherence and obedience to the truth (word of God).

Our Lord, Jesus Christ, said that the Father was always with Him because He (Jesus) always implicitly obeyed the Father (see Jn 8:29).

Therefore, I pray the reader of this book understands and appreciates this book for what it is: an urgent call for spiritual repentance and return to the love of the truth. It is a simple but spiritual message of the truth of the Gospel of Jesus Christ written as revealed and inspired by the Spirit of God: to stir up the saints to wake up and not to be ignorant of the mysteries of the kingdom of God. It is a call for a reality check and self-examination whether we are truly in agreement with God; it is a call to shun the feel-good doctrine and teaching,

What Else?

false prophecy, signs, manipulation, deceit, and lies. The Lord chastises and corrects whom He loves; and as we have read, the judgment of the Lord shall begin at His sanctuary. It must be obvious then to the reader that this book is not intended to entertain anyone, but to get God's children to mourn and repent and return to their first love.

The only way we can walk together and be one with God is to be in spiritual agreement with Him, and this agreement is only possible through perfect love and implicit obedience. These are the two keys that can unlock the kingdom door (Jesus).

I could not write any differently, neither is it possible for me to compromise the words and teachings of the Lord, for who would do that and not be cursed? I do not write so as to make the best-selling list, for the best seller is the undiluted word of God. For the Lord who called me said to me, "I have called you for one purpose only—to go and prepare for the coming of the Lord. I will send you to my churches to go and stir them to examine themselves if they are truly born of Me and now ready, for My coming is nearer at hand. I will teach and reveal to you the mysteries of the kingdom. You must live what I teach you and teach others exactly the same, lest you will be brought under condemnation." So, Lord, I obey. Come, oh Lord, come, please have mercy on us Your children. Therefore, as the Holy Spirit says, "Today, if you will hear His voice, do not harden your hearts as in the rebellion" (Heb 3:7-8).

To God Almighty alone, the only living God, be all the glory now and forevermore. Amen.

Index

A

Aaron 54
Abednego (one of the three Jewish men) 170
Abishai 100, 168
Abner (commander of King Saul's army) 99
Abraham 70, 85, 89, 95, 171-3
Adam 35-6, 40, 138
adultery 30, 35, 37, 126, 152, 162, 167, 187
Africa 24, 46, 50, 62, 70, 89, 99, 111, 115, 124, 129, 136, 171
Ahab (king) 39-40
Amalekites 169
Ammonites 109
Ananias 163
Andrew (Peter's brother) 84

anger 36, 66, 110-14, 132
arguments 32-4
atonement 139 *see also* spiritual foundation: reconciliation
attitude, spiritual 67, 103, 114, 134 *see also* God: born of

B

Bathsheba 39, 162
Bilhah (Rachel's maid) 177
bitterness 112, 123, 125, 132, 134, 142-3 *see also* unforgiveness
blessings 35, 67, 86, 99, 114, 134-5, 156, 159, 165-6, 175, 178-80, 182
body, spiritual 56, 65-6 *see also* God: born of

bondage 31, 49, 58-9, 61-5, 93, 125, 131

C

Cain 101
calamities 108
Canaanites 173
charity 139, 141
commandments (*see also* doctrines) 57, 76, 82-3, 90-1, 100, 127, 129, 144, 158, 162
condemnation 22, 61, 96, 126-7, 193 *see also* judgment
congregations 63, 71, 86, 89, 99, 115, 129, 134, 136, 180
conscience (*see also* spiritual foundation) 17-18, 27, 31, 35, 59, 92, 140, 142, 144, 189

D

darkness 28, 34, 58-9, 61, 70-1, 77, 95, 128, 140, 183
David (king) 35, 39-40, 95, 100, 162, 168-9, 172, 184
death 32, 39, 47, 62-3, 65, 88-90, 98-101, 108, 113, 116, 126, 135, 139, 150, 155-6, 173
deceit 16, 64, 102, 116, 187-8, 191, 193 *see also* lies, manipulation
demonstration 15, 43, 85, 87, 95, 126, 139, 145, 159, 170, 175
devil 31-2, 59, 63-5, 70, 97, 100, 114, 144-5, 154, 160-1, 176-8, 182, 192
doctrines 28, 41, 48-9, 56, 71, 92-3, 97, 102, 116-18, 124-5, 165, 183, 185, 187-9

E

Edom 100
Egypt 49, 172-3
Eli 60
enemies 16, 33, 49, 56, 64, 67-8, 77, 91, 93, 95-100, 102, 108-9, 124, 131, 139, 144-5
envy 116, 119-20, 176, 188
eternal life (*see also* keys of life) 16, 18, 21, 27, 44, 51, 82, 107, 179, 186
Eve 35-6, 40
evildoers 70, 96, 99

Index

F

faith   21, 72, 101, 105, 117-18, 189
Father (*see also* God; Holy Spirit; Jesus Christ)   9, 17-18, 46-7, 52, 63, 92, 96-7, 137, 139, 150, 154, 179
fear, spiritual   58, 64-5
fig tree   43, 185
four spiritual foundations   16, 25
freedom   61, 64

G

Gentiles   57, 70, 163-4, 179
God   9-10, 12, 15-24, 27-49, 51-8, 60-73, 75-7, 81-6, 88-104, 106-14, 116-21, 123-45, 149-72, 174-93
   born of   9, 16-17, 20, 24, 51-5, 57-8, 65-7, 76-7, 93, 95-6, 110-14, 124, 133-4, 139-40, 151-2, 178
   fear of   31, 119, 143, 159, 168
   hunger for   18, 46, 71, 81, 83-90, 175
   kingdom of   1, 3, 9-10, 17, 20-4, 34, 48-9, 75-6, 118, 136, 142-4, 159, 170-2, 175-6, 178-9, 191-2
   Spirit of   15, 18, 24, 27-8, 35, 52-3, 57, 61, 66-7, 73, 96, 99, 103-4, 108, 119-20, 145
   word of   64-5, 72, 102, 141, 154, 181, 183, 185, 192
gradualism   34

H

hatred (*see also* hypocrisy)   92, 98, 100, 102-3, 110, 117, 119, 125, 127, 134
heart, spiritual   56, 124, 128, 133, 143 *see also* God: born of
heresy   96, 99
Herod (king)   141
Holy Ghost Fire   99
Holy Spirit   15, 36, 46, 98-9, 111-14, 125, 131, 133, 140, 154, 193
hypocrisy   70, 103, 189
hypocrites   43, 60, 102-3, 119, 123, 151

I

Israel   39, 60, 88, 95, 100, 109, 135, 158, 171, 173, 176, 180, 184-5

J

Jacob 88, 135, 166, 171-2, 174-5, 177
Jerusalem 68, 130, 135, 185
Jesus Christ 21, 24, 27, 44, 62, 73, 75, 91-2, 97, 102, 107, 126, 138, 141, 150, 188-90
Jews 54, 57, 69-70, 98, 163, 190
Joab 99
John (apostle) 31, 84, 106, 158, 183, 188
John the Baptist 27, 99
Jonathan (son of King Saul) 95
Joseph (son of Jacob) 95, 135, 166-8, 171-3
Joshua 64, 130, 156-8, 173, 180
Judah (son of Jacob) 6, 109, 171-7, 184-5
judgment 40, 57, 63, 67, 83, 85, 96, 100, 113, 117, 119, 127, 137, 149, 181, 190-1

K

keys of life
  love 17, 79
    of God 82-3
    of others 105
  obedience 6, 10, 17-18, 21, 46, 56, 58, 65, 71, 75-6, 102-3, 106, 149-55, 157-9, 178-9, 192-3

L

Lazarus 89-90
Leah (one of Jacob's two wives) 174-7
lesson 35, 134, 176
Levi (son of Leah and Jacob) 174
lies 16, 64, 102, 116, 140, 187, 189, 191, 193
Lord of Hosts *see* God

M

Maker *see* God
manipulation 64, 116, 187, 191, 193
Mary Magdalene 86-7, 89
Meshach 170
mind, spiritual 56-7, 59, 120, 125 *see also* God: born of
ministry 33, 142, 191
miracles 44, 46, 71, 157, 178-9
mission 126-7, 138-40, 142
Moabites 109

Index

Moses 39, 54, 95, 156-7, 168, 180

N

Naboth 39
Nathan 162
Nebuchadnezzar (king) 170
new spirit 54, 56, 67-8, 94, 103, 125, 128
New Testament 37, 97
Nicodemus 72, 152

P

Paul (apostle) 31, 33-4, 47-8, 58, 94, 97, 99, 101, 117, 120, 126, 161, 166, 186, 188, 190-1
perfect love (*see also* heart, spiritual) 18, 56, 65, 76-7, 95, 97, 102, 107, 123, 139, 149, 160-1, 178-9, 193
Peter (apostle) 31, 84, 87, 107, 128, 163, 168
Pharaoh 54, 168
Phares 173
Pharisees 60, 70-2, 102-3, 119
Philistines 100
Pontius Pilate 141
punishment 36, 38-9, 101, 162

R

Rachel (one of Jacob's two wives) 174, 176-7
reciprocity 88-9 *see also* God: hunger for
relationship 16-17, 23-4, 27-8, 41-2, 44, 52, 54, 56, 71, 81, 84, 86, 89-90, 123, 138, 178-9
resentment 99, 125, 127-8, 132, 134, 142-3, 176
resolution 30
restitution 37-8 *see also* spiritual foundation: repentance
restoration 28, 37-8, 138
resurrection 46-7, 62, 87-8, 98
Reuben (first son of Leah and Jacob) 174
righteousness 25, 44-5, 47, 49, 53-4, 61, 65-6, 71, 85, 93, 97-8, 110, 139, 159-61, 168, 179
rooster 63-4

S

Sabbath 87
salvation 46-8, 107, 126, 135, 189

Samuel 57, 60, 162
Sapphira 163
Saul (king) 57, 95, 99-100, 126, 135, 161-2, 168
Sceva 182
scribes 60, 70-1, 102-3
scriptures 24, 29, 32, 37-8, 47-8, 52-4, 57, 65-6, 72-3, 86-7, 100-1, 103, 113-14, 141, 163, 179-83
Simeon (Leah and Jacob's second son) 174
sin 17, 28-34, 37, 39, 47, 49, 65, 72, 128, 132, 165
  first reaction to 35
  fourth reaction to 36
  second reaction to 35
  third reaction to 36
sincerity 18, 140, 142, 144, 159, 161
Solomon (king) 155, 158
spiritual foundation
  agreement 17, 29, 41, 43-4, 46, 151, 178, 193
  forgiveness 17, 25, 27-8, 35, 37-9, 56, 103, 123, 125-9, 133-4, 136-8, 142-3, 189
  reconciliation 17, 25, 103, 123-6, 128, 133, 136-42, 145

repentance 17, 22-3, 25, 27-30, 35, 37-8, 47, 60, 85, 127, 189, 192
Sunday 116

T

Tamar 173
test 49, 68, 81-3, 105-6, 108, 110-11, 134, 167, 169, 183
transformation 9, 52-3, 167
transgression 29, 35-6, 39, 56, 133, 164-5
truth 10, 15-17, 21-5, 31-2, 34, 44, 46, 48-9, 61-2, 66-8, 72-3, 93-4, 118-20, 155, 181, 183-92
two spiritual lessons 82

U

unbelievers (*see also* evildoers) 18, 35, 53-4, 57, 69, 107, 111, 117, 133, 142
understanding, spiritual 52, 75, 141
unforgiveness 123, 127-32, 134, 136 *see also* sin
Uriah the Hittite 39, 162

V

vanity 155
vengeance 96-7, 99-101, 103, 114
victory, spiritual 18, 160-1 *see also* God: born of

W

willpower 41

Z

Zacchaeus 37, 89
Zerubbabel 94